How to Have a Happy Family Life

D0511404

How to Have a Happy Family Life

Suzie Hayman

DUDLEY PUBLIC LIBRARIES	
000000552209	
Bertrams	23/10/2012
306.85	£10.99
	COS

Hodder Education

338 Euston Road, London NW1 3BH.

Hodder Education is an Hachette UK company

First published in UK 2012 by Hodder Education

Copyright © 2012 Suzie Hayman

The moral rights of the author have been asserted

Database right Hodder Education (makers)

The Teach Yourself name is a registered trademark of Hachette UK.

All rights reserved. No part of this publication may be reproduced, stored in a retrieval system or transmitted in any form or by any means, electronic, mechanical, photocopying, recording or otherwise, without the prior permission in writing of Hodder Education, or as expressly permitted by law, or under terms agreed with the appropriate reprographic rights organization. Enquiries concerning reproduction outside the scope of the above should be sent to the Rights Department, Hodder Education, at the address above.

You must not circulate this book in any other binding or cover and you must impose this same condition on any acquirer.

British Library Cataloguing in Publication Data: a catalogue record for this title is available from the British Library.

10 9 8 7 6 5 4 3 2 1

The publisher has used its best endeavours to ensure that any website addresses referred to in this book are correct and active at the time of going to press. However, the publisher and the author have no responsibility for the websites and can make no guarantee that a site will remain live or that the content will remain relevant, decent or appropriate.

The publisher has made every effort to mark as such all words which it believes to be trademarks. The publisher should also like to make it clear that the presence of a word in the book, whether marked or unmarked, in no way affects its legal status as a trademark.

Every reasonable effort has been made by the publisher to trace the copyright holders of material in this book. Any errors or omissions should be notified in writing to the publisher, who will endeavour to rectify the situation for any reprints and future editions.

Hachette UK's policy is to use papers that are natural, renewable and recyclable products and made from wood grown in sustainable forests. The logging and manufacturing processes are expected to conform to the environmental regulations of the country of origin.

www.hoddereducation.co.uk

Cover image © Uros Petrovic - Fotolia

Typeset by Cenveo Publisher Services.

Printed in Great Britain by CPI Group (UK) Ltd, Croydon, CR0 4YY.

Contents

Acknowledgements

Thanks to The Old Vice, as usual – couldn't do it without him, and to Simon Walsh, indefatigable Press and PR manager at Family Lives, for keeping me informed, keeping me amused and keeping me on my toes.

Meet the author

Welcome to *How to Have a Happy Family Life*!

I trained as a teacher, doing a Graduate Certificate in Education, and worked for the Family Planning Association and then Brook Advisory Centres as press and information officer before becoming a freelance journalist. My first column as an agony aunt was with *Essentials* magazine, then *Woman's Own*. I've been a columnist for, amongst others, BBC Health Online, the Saturday *Guardian* and *The Times* and am now agony aunt for *Woman* magazine. I trained with Relate to become a counsellor, and with Triple P (Positive Parenting Programme) to become an accredited parenting educator. I am a spokesperson and trustee for Family Lives, the major UK parenting charity, and a trustee of The Who Cares Trust, for 'looked after' children. I'm one of the founding agony aunts in the Kids In The Middle alliance, lobbying for increased support for children caught up in family breakdown, and have edited the KITM website. I make frequent appearances on national and local television and radio, as a counsellor and agony aunt, and presented my own series on BBC1, *Stepfamilies*. This will be my twenty-ninth published book and I write features, mainly on relationships, parenting, counselling, health and sex matters, for a wide range of national magazines, newspapers and organizations including Family Lives, the NSPCC, One Parent Families, and the Family Planning Association. I am regularly asked to give expert comment in national and local media and to speak at conferences and to give seminars on a wide range of issues to do with relationships and parenting.

Suzie Hayman

Introduction

We often say that happiness is important. Parents may insist that they'd rather their children were happy than successful, that all that matters is for them to be content. We wish each other Happy Birthday or Happy Festivity, whether it's Christmas or Chanukah or whatever. The Pursuit Of Happiness is seen as a human right – it's written into the American Constitution. Yet, in our everyday behaviour we actually pay little attention to the importance of happiness, and make few concessions to pursuing it. When, in recent times, politicians and commentators have suggested it might be desirable to elevate happiness to a more important status in our lives, the general response was mockery, or accusations of the idea being akin to trying to impose a Nanny State. What appears to be of overriding importance in our society is what sort of job you have, how much you earn and what you can buy to demonstrate your status and wealth. Having a job is seen as important, but not as a way of learning, practising and indeed enjoying skills, but as a way of earning the cash to do other things, and of placing you in society. In the UK we have a culture of long hours, the longest in Europe. It's not enough to say this is because of the recession and people's fears of being made redundant – it started long before that happened.

Long hours at work might not be such an issue if it was because we loved our work, were effective in it and benefitted from our working time. There's a wealth of research which shows that many people derive no pride or pleasure from their work, and that those of us working long hours find it impinges most destructively on those aspects of our life that do benefit us most – our relationships, our families and our social networks. Apparently working three hours over the standard day doubles your risk of depression. So excessive working hours are not even good for employers; they are a false economy. And they can be devastating for us and our families. When people look back at the end of their lives, whether in old age or as a result of premature terminal illness, nobody says 'I wish I'd worked longer hours'. Most do, however, say 'I wish I'd spent more time with my family and friends'. In fact, the sort of regrets commonly expressed at such times all hinge around more connection, more self-development, more contentment. More happiness, indeed.

In the UK we are beginning to look at whether we can measure happiness and, having arrived at some way of calculating a National Wellbeing Index, whether we can support or encourage it. Surveys in the UK and the US show that people are no happier now than in the 1950s, despite massive economic growth. In a recent survey in the UK three quarters of respondents said they rated their satisfaction with life at 7 or more out of 10. That might suggest we have little cause for concern. But almost 6 in 10 also said they felt anxious and that their work/life balance was not ideal. And we also know that trust is a major determinant of happiness in a society. The percentage of people who say 'Most people can be trusted' is only 30 per cent of people in the UK and US, compared to 60 per cent some 40 years ago. But in Scandinavia the level is still over 60 per cent, and these are the happiest countries too.

And what about our children – are they happy? A few years ago UNICEF produced a report on child wellbeing in the majority of economically advanced nations of the world. The report measured and compared overall child wellbeing across six dimensions: material wellbeing, health and safety, education, peer and family relationships, behaviours and risks, and young people's own subjective sense of their own wellbeing. In total, 40 separate indicators of child wellbeing – from relative poverty and child safety, to educational achievement to drug abuse – were brought together in this overview to present a picture of the lives of children.

Child wellbeing was found to be at its highest in the Netherlands, Sweden, Denmark and Finland. The United Kingdom and the United States were in the bottom of the rankings. The report showed that there was little relationship between a country's gross domestic product (GDP) – the measure of a country's overall economic output – and the wellbeing of its children. Instead, the range of indicators measured healthy living and risky behaviour – the percentage of young people who eat breakfast daily, fruit daily, who exercise, who are overweight; the percentage of 15-year-olds who smoke, who have had sex, who used condoms last time they had sex, who have had a baby; of 11-, 13- and 15-year-olds who have been drunk, who use cannabis, who have been in a fight, who have been bullied. The UK ranked 21st.

The report looked at relationships with family and friends; the percentage of children who eat their main meal with their parents more than once a week, who say their parents spend time 'just talking' with them, who find other children and young people kind and helpful. The UK ranked 21st.

The report also looked at what young people say about their lives; how they rated their own health, whether they liked school, how happy they were on a scale of 0 to 10 and whether they felt lonely, left out, awkward. They looked at whether children had been bullied or been in a fight recently. The UK ranked 20th.

Unhappiness and conflict in families have dire effects. But it's not just serious conflict in a family or between couples that causes harm. Anger and violent disagreements can be like explosions, forcing families apart and doing considerable and often obvious damage. But constant low-level conflict can be as harmful as cancer, eating away at the bonds between family members and destroying their own self-esteem and confidence. It's a bit like low-level toothache or back pain; each moment may not be disastrous in itself, but taken as a whole and over a period of time, it can be overwhelming.

Families are not just a married man and woman and 2.4 dependent children. They are all shapes and sizes and all ages. There is a wide range of groups who can and should quite rightly see themselves as families. Families in which a parent lives on their own with children, or raises them in co-operation with a parent who lives elsewhere; stepfamilies; families where two adults caring for children are same sex... Families also extend across several generations, grandparents being particularly vital members.

In trying to put our finger on what does and does not contribute to happiness in our family, and nudging ourselves towards the joyful end of the spectrum, it helps to understand how we tick. Why is it that some people find it easy to get on with others, and some seem to lurch from relationship to relationship, endlessly repeating the same unhappy scenario of conflict and misery? Why is it that in one family peace and co-operation can reign while in the next parents and kids appear to always be at each other's throats?

Whether it's nature or nurture that mostly drives us the reality is that the way we work, and therefore the way our families work, can often be understood, predicted and plotted. We can tease out, unpack and see how and why we do what we do, and feel what we feel. And if we can understand why, we can often make changes when what is happening is less than ideal. It might go without saying that this can be vital in families, or in individual lives, with serious conflict or major unhappiness. But it can be important even when you and your family are simply 'getting by'. In many families low-grade conflict is accepted as normal, as is low-grade stress. But both are not just uncomfortable, they are destructive and painful and ultimately immensely damaging. Understanding yourself and the ties that connect you to those around you, and the divisions that make those ties uncomfortable or distressing, can be a first step to transforming your own life and the lives of those with whom you interact.

Of course you can't solve all relationship and family problems – we assume because we are problem-solving animals that all problems have a solution, and that sometimes simply isn't true. But even the experience of having to say 'Actually, there's little we can do about that...' is positive and protective. Often understanding what is the question, even if you don't have a neat answer, tends to move you on. And when you know what you can't change you can then concentrate on the issues you can.

BUT...a word on parenting advice and parenting books, before we go any further. I hope it's both inspiring and reassuring for you to recognize that you can have the best intentions and do all you can to follow best practice, and sometimes fall off that pedestal. You can be mindful, skilful, tolerant and understanding and do your very best to parent your child in such a way as to foster their development and maximize their happiness. And every so often you'll lose it. You'll forget all about being the parent you wish to be and do all the things you swore you'd never do – shout, snap, be impatient, abrupt and unfair. And will it scar your children for life? It's unlikely, as long as it is an aberration and you're doing your best. Acquiring the skills I and other parenting advisors suggest can take time and effort, and since you're often unravelling years of learning to do it in other ways it can feel odd and awkward. Pushed to the limit it's understandable you may not be able to use these skills at a moment's notice. Remind yourself that failure is another chance to learn – it's OK to fail because that often gives us even more reason to see how the new ways really do work better. So dust yourself off, and keep on trying. Positive parenting skills take practice, but they do work.

1

··

The couple

In this chapter you will learn:
- *Why happiness is important*
- *Why focusing on the couple relationship can make a family happy*
- *How and why we choose a particular partner*
- *How to audit your relationship*

Starting with the couple

Families start with the couple. If you share your life with somebody else, your shared happiness is at the root of your individual contentment, self-esteem and self-confidence. It's true that we could all probably point to people who are in a relationship and yet seem to be utterly selfish, looking after Number 1 with little appreciation or care for their partner or the other people around them. They may assert that yes, they are indeed happy. I would argue their apparent happiness is on very shaky foundations. It's certainly not a model to envy or copy. We are interdependent – our wellbeing rests on our fostering and supporting the parallel wellbeing of those closest to us. But how often do we forget this? Research suggests that only 3 in 10 parents think their own relationship is important to their children. In a dramatic reversal, 7 in 10 children say whether their parents are happy with each other is of vital importance to them. So, if for no other reason than to add to the sum total of happiness for your children, couples need to foster, strengthen and cultivate their own relationships. And you need to do that from the very beginning of your partnership. Because, of course, there is another reason you should do it, apart from for your children. You should do it for each other, and for yourselves.

Happiness is good for you

Why is happiness important?

▶ Happy people are more likely to be in a relationship and for that relationship to be lasting. Married people live longer and are healthier than the single or divorced.
▶ Happy people are healthier and feel less stressed.
▶ Happy people have less conflict, in the family and in the workplace. They tend to seek solutions and be more optimistic and 'can do' than unhappy people.
▶ Happy people are less likely to suffer frequent niggly illnesses.
▶ Happy people tend to feel more energetic – they learn faster, whether at school or at work, and co-operate better with those around them.
▶ Happy people are more altruistic and help those around them. This sets up a 'ripple effect' where people who have been helped and supported pass it on, so widening the pool of happiness.
▶ Happy people tend to get the breaks – other people like them and help them out while they, being more optimistic, tend to see opportunities where less happy people might not.
▶ Happiness feels good.

Finding your other half

To cultivate your store of happiness and make your family a happy one you first need to understand how people choose a partner. How do you fall in love, with whom and why? We talk about opposites attracting, about love at first sight and often say all you need is love. But how do we understand and explain the process of mutual attraction? Sometimes we seem to take an instant dislike or at least strike up an instant hostile spark with the person we eventually settle down with – the stuff of all good movies. Sometimes, it's an instant connection. But why do some people seem to find themselves drawn, again and again, to people with whom they have damaging, abusive relationships while others fall for the good guys?

FALLING IN LOVE

In some cultures a lot of store is set on the process of falling in love as the best guide to your choosing a partner. You aren't expected nor do you expect yourself, at least initially, to think about whether they are suitable on a whole range of social, economic or personality issues. All that seems to matter is how you feel. Do they make your heart race, your palms go wet, your mouth dry? Do they sexually interest you? Are you, in short, falling in love?

Insight

Love has been described as a chemically induced period of insanity, and one that can only last a matter of months. In fact, love can be divided into three distinct phases, one of which is short lived, another of which can last longer and the third of which can last a lifetime.

What are the three phases of love?

Falling in love is an overwhelming emotion – that insanity that can have you making a fool of yourself and doing things you'd never do in your right mind. When you fall in love you want to be with the person of your affections as often as possible, you think about them all the time and may talk about them to your friends and family at every excuse. When you fall in love there can be a certain amount of fantasy involved – the image you have of your love object may not be entirely accurate. Falling in love can be triggered as soon as you meet someone or come upon you over a period – usually a short period – of time. It's very like the 'rush' from taking a drug, since it is a reaction to hormones rushing round your body, and not really something that is sustainable for long periods.

Being in love is the next stage, and a far more settled state of affairs as you get to know your partner as a genuine individual. The adrenaline kick of falling in love will recede and instead of the frenetic excitement you experience a quieter, more relaxed emotion. The dramatic highs may be fewer but the fear and insecurity of not knowing whether the person you love returns your emotion can also be gone. Being in love is the period when you and your partner learn about each other and about your relationship – how you both tick, how you fit together, how it works.

Loving is the final stage and it is the emotion we feel when we know a partner through and through, can see failings for what they are and still love them. The intense highs and lows of falling or even being in love can fade but what is left is a sense of commitment, of connection and interdependence – each partner both supports and leans on the other, has trust, respect and intimacy.

LOVE AT FIRST SIGHT

The ideas of Love At First Sight and Mr/Ms Right do have some basis, and both are part of an explanation for how and why we fall in love.

Whether we realize it or not, we choose the people we fall in love with and with whom we form relationships. Falling in love, even 'love at first sight', is the result of complex decision-making, not a matter of haphazard chance. To all intents and purposes all you have to go on when you catch sight of someone, or are introduced to them, is their appearance. What another person looks like is important to some extent, but this doesn't mean that we fall for appearance and appearance alone. Or, more properly, it isn't whether they are conventionally good looking or come up to the standards of the day in being 'hot or not' that matters. What is going on in that first encounter is that your unconscious rather than your conscious mind is making a very quick but astonishingly thorough assessment.

Insight

Think of the human brain as a super-computer, able to consider and examine an amazing amount of information in less time than it takes to blink. There's a lot more to instant attraction than meets the eye. What actually happens is that we all carry within us a blueprint of the ideal partner. Think of it as a checklist, or a jigsaw in which we have half of the pieces, or half the workings of a mechanical clock.

BLUEPRINTS

How do we come to carry this blueprint? It's the result of our own background, our upbringing and development. All your relationships and experiences as you go through life, from birth (and actually even before that) contribute to a map of your needs, beliefs, abilities, characteristics, personality, traits and values. What you see and experience tells you who you are and what you're worth. What you see and experience tells you who your partner should be and how they might fulfil you and fit in with you. You might think you're attracted to Tall Dark and Handsome, or Small, Blond and Cute, and yet repeatedly fall for people almost the opposite of that. The reason you find them irresistible is because something in their looks or their behaviour calls to you. It may remind you of someone, or something, that says 'This is familiar, this is right' and it may do so in the most unexpected ways.

Your past experience tells you, for instance, that men with a quirky smile are safe – because your dad who was loving and kind had one. Or women who laugh outright are adorable – because your mother who was caring and attentive did that. All the way through your childhood (and on into adulthood, but childhood messages are the most important) your mind will go on building up the picture of the person you are looking for.

Insight

Sexual stereotypes in our society insist that men and women see love in different ways. In fact it's been said that romance is the price men pay to get sex while sex is the price women pay to get romance. Most men would have you believe that they are interested in conquest and sex and prefer to leave the slushy stuff to women. But those who deal with men on an emotional level, such as counsellors and agony aunts, believe that there are more similarities than differences between men and women. Women are just as interested in sex as men and men are just as emotionally needy as women. What both sexes want is intimacy, connection and closeness, and both sexes undoubtedly fall in love.

THE UNCONSCIOUS CHECKLIST

When you meet or see someone, your unconscious mind spins through a checklist; it's as if it joins the dots that paints the picture of what your life experience thinks your partner should look like.

After a certain number of ticks and crosses, you may write the person off – they don't measure up. What this feels like to you is simply indifference – you may like them or you may dislike them, but they don't ring your bell. Or, you may feel drawn to them, powerfully or with just the glimmerings of interest. Or, as in all the best films and books, you may have quite strong negative feelings of hostility or dislike, thinking them stuck up or arrogant or too full of themselves. This in itself may be a form of sexual attraction, when part of your mind resists the feelings, or is taken by surprise at the reaction that another part is having.

What is really interesting is that you may think only surface details can be considered this way. So you wouldn't be surprised to learn that some people have a thing about blondes with an easy smile while others go for smouldering, brooding redheads. But this blueprint can lead you to falling for less obvious characteristics, such as a tendency to cheat, a shared history of abuse or the fact that both of you lost members of your family at the same time in childhood. Such parallels in partners' backgrounds are remarkably common and frequently are not realized by the couple until well into their relationship.

THE IMPORTANCE OF FAMILIARITY

When you meet someone who does tick many of your boxes there is often an intense feeling of familiarity and of their somehow fitting with you. Some of that will be the familiarity of shared experiences – of growing up in similar circumstances with similar people. This is why arranged marriages can work very well. Partly this can be a matter of expectations. Couples in a culture in which this is the norm do not anticipate, or perhaps even value, falling in love as part of the deal, but look on the marriage as being about family alliances. Their success may also be because the basis for most good relationships is that you share a lot of background and so understand each other – you're familiar with all the things your partner is also familiar with. This is then bolstered by shared beliefs in the way relationships and family work and what you should expect. But many couples in such a situation also find themselves drawn to the partner chosen for them. This is because the chemistry that makes sexual attraction is all about recognition and acquaintance. You have in common the food you eat, the festivals you celebrate, the places you go and the things you do. That in itself triggers feelings of safety and comfort, which lead to intimacy.

Those shared experiences may not only be the obvious ones of what you both might have encountered in your families, communities, and schools. They may also be more personal and often concealed aspects of your life. You might discover you both went through some pivotal event at the same age – a loss, a realization, or an incident. There is often something there that draws you together even if you'd think it wouldn't show, and you might have forgotten it, not thought it significant or just not got round to talking about it. You might also find your position in the family – the youngest daughter of three girls, the oldest son of two boys – pushes you towards your partner.

Insight

Your birth order – whether you are eldest or youngest (and male or female) – has a lot to do with why brothers and sisters can turn out to have such different personalities. And it can have a significant effect on who you might choose as a partner. If you're the youngest of three, you don't look at life in the same way as you would if you were an only child. If you've got two brothers, you react differently to men and women than you would if you had just one sister.

THE ONE PERSON FOR YOU

The feeling of familiarity and the sense of a partner somehow fitting in with you that often comes when you meet someone who ticks your boxes is where the Mr/Ms Right myth comes in. There is a problem however in thinking there will be only one person who will have this effect on you. Among all the thousands of people you will meet in a lifetime there will actually be a considerable number who would fit your blueprint. Just think about it – if you've a hundred points that are to be ticked or crossed, there must be many people that you meet and know who would score in some of those categories. It's not unreasonable to expect that half a dozen people in your immediate vicinity can rack up a high enough score to hit the jackpot, even though each of them gets ticks and crosses in totally different boxes. We tend to get considerable confusion, for instance, where different people score highly in totally different if not opposing ways. For instance, one may make your pulse race but lose points on some issues – not having similar political views for instance, or being thoughtless about your feelings. Another produces a warm glow, because they are kindness and thoughtfulness personified, but feel boring and too predictable to you. Which do you choose?

The problem with the Mr/Ms Right myth is that it encourages us to misinterpret our reactions to other people. Falling in love, establishing a relationship, marrying and having kids does not render you immune to the charms of new people. We tend to assume that if we've fallen in love, we must have found the one and only person we can pair up with. We also think that as soon as a relationship is established, it acts as a sort of vaccination against sexual or romantic attraction. You feel that no-one will notice you henceforth and you certainly won't notice anyone else. This, of course, is far from the truth. But when someone in a relationship finds themselves aroused by another man or woman, the myth of Mr/Ms Right leads them to believe that what has actually happened is that they got it wrong the first time. Their established partner must be Mr/Ms Wrong, the love they felt must be an illusion and they should be with the new attraction.

Essential points to consider

▶ Families start with a couple, and the happiness of that couple is the foundation of family contentment

▶ Love at first sight is a lot more complex than it sounds

▶ The blueprint or map that describes your perfect partner is built up mainly from experiences in childhood

▶ There is no Mr or Ms Right – hundreds of people could probably tick the same number of boxes. It's all down to which one you find first – and whether having made your choice you're prepared to work at your relationship with that one or throw away the investment.

THE IMPORTANCE OF CHILDHOOD EXPERIENCE

Partners and people who attract us do so because they fulfil a need, or needs, that often go unrecognized in our conscious minds. Sometimes, the need is to make right something that might have gone wrong in our childhood. Events and relationships in childhood are vitally important. I've talked about it setting up that blueprint, that checklist or map, for what you will find essential in a partner. What happens to you as a child is like having a script written for you, for later life.

If your parents were loving and supportive, were there when you needed them but gave you plenty of encouragement to stand on your own two feet, you are likely to grow up with a script that tells you you're a worthwhile person who deserves to love and be loved, and can be competent and capable. You will find yourself being attracted to partners who resemble the best in your parents. And this may not only be in their behaviour, their quirks of personality but also in their appearance. Some researchers suggest that your ideal person is someone who actually strongly resembles yourself. It is noticeable how often couples look as if they could be related. And, indeed, how, more often than can be accounted for by chance, couples names start with the same letter – John and Jane, Peter and Paula.

LOOKING FOR A HAPPIER ENDING

When parents are not able to give you the care you need, and are physically or emotionally absent for all or some of your childhood, the script will be different. You'll still look for a partner who resembles a parent, but with the hope that the story will end on a happier note, with them able to love and care for you and to 'be there' for you. But this so often backfires on you. You'll be choosing someone like the parent who let you down, who is like them and you hope will therefore stand in for them and do it correctly this time. You'll be hoping to rewrite the script but with a happy ending. But, after all, you will in essence be choosing someone like your parent and that will include their inability to fulfil your need. The original didn't do it the first time; the substitute is unlikely to be able to do it the second (or third or fourth) time. And, since not having an adequate model to copy, you yourself may well have no real idea of how to satisfy the same needs in the other person; you may find yourself repeating the same mistakes your parents made with you. This is why relationships, even between couples who love each other, so often encounter problems. And why, if they break up, you can find other, later, relationships going exactly the same way as first ones. Many of our needs remain unchanged over the years, so a new partner may well resemble old ones, both in appearance and in their character and behaviour. They may seem different, and in some ways act differently, but unless you can come to an understanding of what you are really looking for in your partners, you may in essence go on dating, living with or even marrying the same person time after time, and finding dissatisfaction each time.

MARITAL FIT

Counsellors call the way we and our partners slot together 'marital fit'. You can see it in terms of a jigsaw or the cogs of an old-fashioned clockwork watch. Your other half is the person whose pieces fit in with yours, who matches. That doesn't mean a person whose tastes are exactly the same as yours. On the contrary, it often means finding the person who fills in your gaps. Love is often more successful when you do have a lot in common, come from similar backgrounds and therefore have similar references. And it does seem as if familiarity is a big draw – the familiarity of shared backgrounds or shared issues. But on an emotional level we often need people who match but don't accord. This is why 'wallflowers' so often link up with 'party animals'. One side of the partnership may have stage fright and be terrified of the thought of being the centre of attention. They fall for a partner who will do it for them – who will dance on tables, be the life and soul, for both of them. In turn, Party Animal chooses Shrinking Violet for their stability, calmness and quietness, to be the still centre of the relationship.

REWRITING THE SCRIPT

It also explains why some men and women keep falling in love with people who use and abuse them. Abusive relationships are all about the need to rewrite that script. If a child grows up in a family where there is physical or emotional violence or even where there is an apparently loving but emotionally demanding parent, it will affect how they make their own loving relationships later in life. Sometimes what happens is that they are left with a deep sense of being unworthy. They will seek out partners who behave in much the same way as did the abusive or missing parent. They will expect nothing better from their partner because their experience has convinced them that they are worth nothing more. Sometimes the same pattern will happen but it's because the man or woman will convince themselves that this time they can make a difference. You will find men and women who seek out unfaithful, unloving or even brutal partners, or partners with addictive behaviours such as dependency on drink, drugs or gambling. Each time at the root of their love is the conviction that they can change their partner and what they are doing. Whether they can or not, and it's usually futile, it wouldn't make any difference because the person whose behaviour they really want to change is beyond their reach – that is, their parent, in their past. Even if they were able to make it right in the present by having their partner become as loving and caring as they want, there would still be a sense of loss. The real success, to have gone back in time and made the parent clean up their act, is impossible. The third way that people may react in trying to rewrite their own experience of an abusive relationship in childhood is to become abusive themselves.

PASSING ON BAD FEELINGS

Both men and women can visit exactly the same abuse that they suffered at the hands of their carers upon their own partners or children. The reason for this is quite complex. You would think that if you had suffered pain and humiliation the last thing you would want to do is act that way to someone else. In fact, copying what has happened to you is a recognized coping mechanism. A child who has been hurt will feel a tremendous weight of pain, humiliation and powerlessness. The need will be to get rid of those feelings and one way of doing so is to pass them on to someone else. It's a bit like taking all your negative feelings, wrapping them in a parcel and dumping them in someone else's lap. If you can make someone else feel hurt, humiliated and powerless, you yourself can feel satisfied, strong and in control. The exact reverse, in other words, of the negative feelings you once had. This is why the abused can become abusers and why those who have been smacked and hit in childhood often become the strongest exponents of such behaviour.

Insight

Children always love their parents no matter what their parents do to them – you can't help it. It's hard-wired into you and it comes with the territory. When a parent does something that makes a child feel bad two things happen. One is that the child convinces themselves that it must have happened because they did something wrong and must be at fault, which is where the conviction of unworthiness comes from. The other is that the child is driven to forgive the parent and the best forgiveness is to imitate.

We defend behaviour such as smacking and do it ourselves not really because we think it's right or like it or even think it's an efficient way of behaving. Most parents can see right in front of them that smacking, for instance, does not make children better behaved but increases resentment, anger and pain, and often leads to even worse behaviour. We feel driven to repeat it however in order to forgive our parents for having done it to us. Every child wants the world to make sense and to be stable. To have to accept that our parents or carers had lost the plot and were wrong in what they did is a bit like having to accept we lived on shifting sands. It simply feels so risky we'd rather believe that it was we who were wrong and deserved what happened, however awful.

CHOOSING PRIORITIES

One common human behaviour pattern that really does work against your having a happy relationship is the belief, held especially by women, that you have to be perfect – perfect partner, perfect householder, perfect employee. The truth is that you can't do it all. Often in relationships and in family life you have to get your priorities right. On one level it may give you satisfaction to know you're the person who does everything for your family and your partner – cooks, cleans, plays, earns and pays, and does it all faultlessly. But sometimes you have make decisions that allow you to fulfil the one, most important central thing – to be happy and help your family to be happy. That may mean letting go on some issues – letting the dust bunnies grow under the bed – so you can spend time on others, blowing bubbles and running around in the park with your loved ones. It's all about working out the costs and the benefits. For instance, you may feel you have a moral duty to be the person who cleans in your house. The cost may be that it takes two, three or four hours of your time every week to do so. You and your partner could each work an extra hour each week to earn enough to pay a cleaner (thereby benefitting the finances of that cleaner) and free yourself for two hours of quality time spent with your family. Or, you could make it a game that everyone does a bit, with the reward of time spent together. Or, you could decide to let the dust gather (writer Quentin Crisp said 'There was no need to do any housework at all. After the first four years the dirt doesn't get any worse.'). Whatever your choice the important thing is to make it a choice, recognizing the downsides and upsides of whatever you decide. And once you acknowledge that, you can often look for innovative ways of achieving your aims.

TWELVE TIPS FOR A GOOD RELATIONSHIP

1 Recognize that the buck stops with you – make it personal and take responsibility. Ban the phrases 'It's not my fault', 'Someone should do something' and 'What can I do about it?'.

2 The only measure of your happiness and your life should be yourself – don't compare yourself or those close to you to other people. So what if they seem to be getting by, or thriving, or having to do it another way? What is right for them may not be right for you.

3 See yourself as a continuing project on the way to improvement. Learn new skills, new ideas, new ways of looking at things, for yourself and for your relationship. It's never too late to learn and not only is the result good for you, so is the process and it's fun.

4 It may sound obvious, but make an effort to do the things that make you happy. Whatever rings your bells, do as much of it as you can – with the happiness of others in mind too. It won't increase your own happiness if you spend all your time away from your family indulging your own hobby. But giving yourself and them permission to enjoy individual interests now and again will.

5 Count your pennies. Good budgeting is a vital tool on the path to happiness. Remember Dickens's character Micawber in *David Copperfield*, and what is known as the Micawber Principle; 'Annual income twenty pounds, annual expenditure nineteen pounds nineteen and six, result happiness. Annual income twenty pounds, annual expenditure twenty pounds ought and six, result misery.' Being rich is not the way to happiness, but managing what money you have so you keep out of debt is.

6 Get up and do it. Leaping into action without first assessing the situation isn't sensible. Whatever it is, you need to plan: to understand what's going on and what is needed, to gather information and work out what you are going to do. But none of this has any point unless you are prepared to act, and happiness is often dependent on your actually doing something and taking steps.

7 Stand by what you know is right. It may seem that many of the most successful and thus apparently happy and contented people you see in the news have no principles at all. Cheats, liars, dissemblers and hypocrites often appear to thrive. It's easy to get the impression that values, ethics and morality are optional and, indeed, a decided drag on the good life. But it would seem that

appearances are deceptive. Happiness goes hand in hand with having principles and sticking to them. Good people may not be the richest, but they often are the happiest.

8 Socialize. People who have friends and spend time with them are happier. Online friends can be fun and open a door to possibilities otherwise out of your reach, but there is no substitute for face to face friends, friendships and time together.

9 Put on a happy face. You'd be surprised how often you can cheer yourself up if you're not feeling on top of your game simply by acting it. And smiling at other people is catching – most of the time they'll not only smile back at you, they'll then smile at others and the happiness spreads.

10 Be active. We know that exercise triggers our bodies to produce feel-good hormones. Running or cycling round the block or having a session in the gym gives you a kick, quite apart from the way it makes you feel good because you're fitter, healthier and probably slimmer.

11 Be generous. People who give their time as well as their money to charitable or community causes, who help their friends and family, tend to be happier.

12 Make dates to spend time together, both at home and out, and even schedule times you will be romantic. It might appear to take the spontaneity out of it, but you'll be surprised how effective and enjoyable it can be.

Essential points to consider

- ▶ We often choose partners who represent things in our childhood we wish had been different, hoping that this time we can rewrite the script and make it better.
- ▶ While we choose partners who represent similar backgrounds we may also choose someone who can fill in the gaps – be the party animal for both of you while you are the calm, still centre for both of you.
- ▶ If you always seem to have the bad luck to link up with uncaring or even abusive partners it's worth thinking the pattern through. It may not be luck but the way your script is pushing you – once you're aware of that you can change it.

Changing ourselves

If the people you are likely to fall for, the way you fall in love and the way you manage your relationship and family are predetermined by your childhood experiences, can you make any changes? Are you doomed to repeat that script, whether you like it or not?

It's usually not possible to change someone else. However hard you cry, shout or plead with another person, unless they themselves understand why they behave the way they do and want to be different, you're up against a brick wall. But anyone can change the way they themselves feel and the way they behave. To do so, you need to understand what you do and why you do it. We are all the sum of our pasts, and all the little details of our history and our family's history go to make up the patchwork that is us. Understanding these details can give you the clue to seeing where your partner fits in and why you chose each other. It can also explain the particular points of conflict you may have. Change within a couple obviously works best if both halves see the need, and do the work to understand and to do things differently. But even though you cannot change someone else, changing yourself can have quite profound effects on the way your relationship operates and your partner acts.

Insight
Einstein once said a definition of insanity is doing the same thing over and over again and expecting different results. I'd call it a good definition of an unhappy relationship! Sanity, and a good relationship, may be recognizing the script you're following and making changes in your behaviour, expectations and beliefs to rewrite it.

DIGGING UP THE PAST

What is the point of all this dwelling on the past? Many people feel that dredging up what has happened to us, especially if it is negative or unhappy, is at best a waste of time and at worst not letting bygones be bygones. The reason it is actually important is that however much you might like them to do so, sleeping dogs simply won't lie. What has happened to you in your earlier life, however much you might like to ignore it, has very real effects on your present and on your future life.

It won't go away just because you close your eyes. On the contrary, what it does is colour much of what you do whether you realize it or not. But the past has its strongest effect when we try and forget it because our feelings then pop up at unexpected times in unexpected ways. If you face events and your feelings about them squarely, you get them in perspective and under control.

COPING BEHAVIOUR

There are many ways unhappy experiences in childhood reflect on your ability to manage your relationship as a couple. People who seem unable to commit to love, or leave relationships just when the going gets good, often do so because they are reacting to childhood losses. Loss is a painful experience that leaves you feeling powerless. One way of coping is to avoid being vulnerable to another person ever again, by refusing to love or by being the one who leaves first. As with abusive behaviour, the person doing it is not aware of how and why they act the way they do. But couples who feel they are supporting each other and in a good and loving relationship may still, without realizing it, be acting out a family script handed down by their parents, who in turn picked it up from theirs. The way you handle conflict or difficulties in your relationship as a couple or in your family is dictated by the way it was done in your family of origin. Some people, for instance, find the idea of conflict terrifying. 'We've never had an argument in our relationship' may be a true boast, but it's often not because the couple or the family had no disagreements. What you get in some families is an unspoken agreement to 'sit on' certain feelings and certain behaviours. Anger and jealousy, for example, may be emotions that feel far too terrifying and potentially damaging to allow in your life. So you might, unconsciously, decide to ignore them – to banish them. To make sure they never come in, you choose a partner who feels the same way. But that doesn't mean you can't and don't feel those emotions. What it often means is that they simmer underneath the surface. Because you've ignored them neither of you has learnt to handle those emotions very well. But ignoring such powerful and fundamental emotions is a bit like brushing dirt under the carpet. Sooner or later there's a bump big enough to trip over. And sooner or later, you trip over the bump, or the emotion finally bursts out and because neither you nor the partner you've chosen has learnt to handle such feelings, it's unpleasant and difficult.

GETTING CONTROL

If you think of falling in love as just something 'that happens', out of
the blue, you can be forgiven for feeling that it's a situation out of your
control. You'd then also feel that once love changes – a relationship
becomes humdrum, a love goes stale or even appears to die – that too
would be something about which you were powerless. Perhaps now
you can see that love isn't random, which also means that with a bit of
understanding, you can be in the driving seat. Once you can grasp the
foundations of your own relationship, you can shore them up if they've got
a bit shaky. If you want to keep your relationship alive, you can also use
your knowledge to return to those first principles whenever you choose.

Exercise

Having a happy relationship is all about being aware of
what drives you and what you expect and need, in your life
and in your relationship. It's then about communicating,
negotiating and compromising with your partner to find
the best for both of you. The earlier on in a relationship
you set up the practice, as a routine, of touching base, the
better and happier you will be. Stay in touch by taking the
time to summon up what got you there in the first place.
Whether your relationship is in its first year, or twentieth
plus year, sit down with your partner and tell each other:

▶ What you first noticed about each other
▶ What first attracted you to each other
▶ What you liked doing with each other when you first got
together
▶ What you miss doing and would like to do again
▶ What you like doing now
▶ What new thing you'd like to do with each other

Make a date, this weekend or one evening this week, to
do one of the things you miss doing from the beginning,
like doing now or would like to try. Agree to do this
exercise once a week in future. Take it in turns to choose
something old or new to keep your relationship alive.

FAKING EMOTIONS MAKES IT REAL

If you feel the emotions you once felt are long gone and that such an exercise would be just going through the motions, here's the carrot: you'd be surprised how feigning an emotion swiftly becomes feeling that emotion. This is one of the reasons I'm always so strongly against people 'playing it cool' and not being up-front and honest about how they feel for someone. Playing it cool is playing with fire, of course, because of the dangers of simple misunderstanding. Some people may be bubbling over to pursue you when they think you're unobtainable. Just as many would take the hint, think you're not interested and withdraw. Another reason is that your disdain can spark off similar feelings in the other person. But perhaps the most important reason is that when you play it cool, you often go cool. Conversely, when you play it hot, especially when it's to call to mind very real feelings you once had, you soon find they're there for real again.

> **Insight**
>
> Happiness, whether in a relationship or a family, is something we need to work at. Because the initial feelings may seem spontaneous we often then believe the rest of it should follow spontaneously too and be effortless and instinctive. As we've seen, even those initial feelings of attraction and interest are built on a foundation – just because we don't notice the foundations doesn't mean they're not there. Now you can see your unconscious does a lot of work to create those feelings, you can see it is something we can also work on, to maintain and develop the resulting partnership.

FAMILY SCRIPTS

It often helps to visualize much of what motivates and drives you as a script, written for you by events in your, and your family's, past. Jayden saw a counsellor when his marriage became stressful and unhappy. Under the counsellor's prompting he started to think about his mother and the way they had got on. 'My mother was brilliant – a really beautiful woman who held down a responsible job as well as bringing up three of us when our father left.' But Jayden gradually had to confront the fact that he was also resentful of the attention his mother gave to her job, and to his siblings. He'd married someone just like her – attractive and vibrant, with a job that took up much of her time. And they argued constantly about how much time they could give to each other, but Jayden finally realized that while complaining about it, he also encouraged it. He came to realize he'd chosen his wife for the similarity in his mother, and while trying to change the script he'd also supported it. His wife said the one time she took time off to be at his beck and call, he'd run a mile. She and Jayden co-operated in finding a middle way, so that both could spend quality time together and make each other feel special, while still pursuing careers that both valued.

Insight

Seeing the pattern set by the past as a script, rather than fate or something set in stone, gives you the remedy. Scripts can be rewritten. Once you know the themes that keep popping up in your life and the assumptions that are behind many of those self-fulfilling prophecies, you can change them. If you know you look for people who will let you down because you don't think you deserve better, you can work on and improve your self-esteem. If you repeatedly leave relationships just when the going gets good, you can chase down why you fear intimacy so much and do something about it.

LABELS

There is another part of family scripts that can become important to the way you fall in love. People within families often find themselves bearing labels that are given, or seem to be handed down, to them. These can be nicknames, descriptions or predictions: 'You're like your uncle, he was a rogue too.' Or 'Don't take Bel seriously, she's such a tease', or 'Mark my words, you're going to end up just like your dad – what a waste of time he was.' Sometimes the labels seem complimentary: 'I couldn't do without Sandra, she's a perfect child, so well behaved'. Sometimes they are more damaging 'Look at the way your brother has gone. I don't know what to do about the two of you.'

Exercise: Choosing your own label

Consider with your partner the roles you've assumed or been given. Do you like these roles? Would you like to change? How can you change? Sit down and write out a list of the beliefs you have about yourself. For every negative belief – *I'm no good at organizing, I'm lazy, I'm a useless cook* – fill in something positive – *I'm loyal, I'm funny, I don't give up easily*. Now you have filled in your lists, think about and discuss how, when and why you got these opinions. Who told you that you were good, who told you that you were bad and why? Were they right, and what have you done to fulfil that expectation and keep that label? And most important of all, if the negative list is longer than the positive one, go back with your partner and talk it through to see how many positives you can add.

Samantha was a naughty, wilful, disobedient child. At least she was always considered so, in comparison to her older, more helpful and responsible older sister Anna. Samantha was always told off for being untidy or lazy while Anna was always being praised for being obedient and hardworking. Anna became a nurse, married and had three children. She spends most of her time running around after her family, who know they're not expected to lift a hand at home because good old Mum will do it all, as she always has. Samantha has gone on to be really successful in a setting that requires her to be organized, flexible and very hard working. Her family still sees her as the bad one, though. After trying to call their attention to her achievements, she's given up. Whatever she does she knows they will continue to see her as the untidy, wilful and lazy one.

Good labels are unhelpful too
Being given, and feeling you have to live up to, a 'Good' label can be as destructive as being given a bad one. Either way they get you stuck in a role that you've outgrown or that stifles and undermines you. The problem with labels is twofold: they're straitjackets and they describe the wrong thing. When a person is labelled as lazy, selfish, stupid, what is being said is that's what they are, full stop. They're being told they're not liked for what they are, not what they do, and thus there's no point in even trying to be different because it is them, not their behaviour, that is dislikeable. When you tell yourself you are useless or incompetent or no good, you fix

yourself in being exactly that and give yourself no hope of making any change. Why should your partner make the effort to pick up his dirty shirts, wash the pots or feed the dog? You've said that they are messy, inconsiderate and irresponsible, and cleaning up their act ain't going to change your mind about them. The trick is to start looking at those unattractive aspects as *behaviour* rather than *person*. Not that they are *selfish* but that they are *behaving in a selfish way*. Not that they are *unhelpful*, but that they are *being unhelpful at this particular moment*. Not that they are *inconsiderate* but that *that was an inconsiderate thing to do or say*. Not that you are *stupid*, but that *you mucked up that one time and can do better*. If we stop labelling the person, we have every reason to focus on and consider changing the things that are causing problems.

Insight

You can change the way you see yourself and you can change the way other people who have always known you see you as well. It can take persistence and time but as long as you strongly hold to your own, new perception of yourself, most people will eventually see it. And if they don't, that's their lookout: don't let them affect you.

Relationship audit

You can use an understanding and sharing of your likes and dislikes to inform a relationship audit. An audit is when you examine or inspect something with a view to seeing if it works, if it's valid and if you can improve it or make it more appropriate. You might think of accounts being audited, or a business's practices. Relationships can be audited too, and what that means is giving yourself the opportunity to ask 'Is this working, are we happy, is there anything we can or should do to make it better?' You may need to ask questions about yourself and what you do, about how much you understand yourself and your partner, and how much and how well you communicate. You could do an audit before setting up home together to agree how you're going to manage sharing a space and a life. You could do it before taking the big step of making a more formal agreement – a wedding or civil partnership. You could do it before taking perhaps the even bigger step – before or after a formal commitment! – of having children together. Or you could do it at any stage of a relationship – 1, 10 or 20+ years into it. It's never too late to check out how you're doing and what you might like to do to make your family run more smoothly.

SHINING A LIGHT

When you do an audit you may find there are important aspects of yourself, your relationship and your life together that have gone under the radar – you've never mentioned them or taken some things for granted. You may find some startling similarities – things that bring you together and explain your connection but that you've never had brought out into the open. On the other hand, you may find things that could threaten to derail you, if you don't address them. Doing an audit allows you the chance to build on the pluses and deal with the minuses. But it is powerful stuff and not to be taken lightly. The whole point of the exercise is to dig deep and find out what makes your partnership tick. But it is also designed to help you shine a light on what comes between you – the barriers to communication to honesty and commitment.

BEING MINDFUL

Relationships often get into trouble because either we just drift into it, or spend more time planning one day – a wedding or ceremony – than we do on planning the following years together. Relationships involve so much more than that initial declaration. They deserve more thought and preparation, more skills and application. They deserve a willingness to understand how you and your backgrounds, expectations and values, either mesh or collide. It's not necessarily a mismatch that triggers problems but misunderstandings, and lack of communication. We call this being mindful – focusing on what we feel, what matters, what we would like to do and what we would rather not do. Sharing details can be so illuminating, and helpful because it allows you to be mindful about yourself, and about your partner, rather than just letting time and life and outside influences push you along. Once you know what similarities and dissimilarities you have, once you understand how and why they get in the way or pull you together, you can make choices to strengthen your relationship.

BE CAREFUL

But this does have to come with a warning. Sharing even trivial details about yourselves can be explosive. It may take you by surprise what a powerful effect bringing out details about yourself can be.

Some of those seemingly silly stories of your past, or even putting your finger on how you feel or react in the here and now, can dredge up feelings you might not have expected – of sadness, regret, loss or anger. You may make excuses not to do this exercise, thinking it's silly or useless or even intrusive. The real reason may be that you recognize without realizing it how much it may affect you, and that may be why you feel disinclined to do this exercise. You should certainly respect the possible difficulties, but still go ahead. What you might like to do is put some safeguards in place – an agreed signal to take a break and regroup. And if it does get too hard, rather than an excuse to abandon it, that may be a very good reason to ask for the professional help of a counsellor.

Case study

When Robyn married Bruno she turned down her aunt's offer of some sessions with a counsellor beforehand. The aunt was a therapist and while she couldn't offer to help Robyn herself for ethical reasons, she had realized there were issues that her niece and husband-to-be needed to sort out. But Robyn turned her down saying she had far too much to do with the wedding planning. She also insisted, laughing that 'It would be far too boring if I knew too much about him now – what would we have to talk about later?' Six years later, on the brink of breaking up, she asked for the name of a good counsellor, and one of the techniques the counsellor led them through was a 'getting to know each other' exercise. One of the issues that surprised them was dramatically different ideas about women working, and having children. Robyn felt having career was vital to her self-image and self-confidence, and for that reason was putting off having children. She felt Bruno wouldn't support her going back to work once she took time off to have a baby. In her family, her mother and her sisters all had careers and she felt it was a positive and important part of any family life that women worked. Bruno's mother also worked but it became clear that the message he'd got from his father was that a man wasn't a man if he didn't support his family while his wife stayed at home. His parents had separated when Bruno was 12, and contact with his father was sporadic and difficult. But Bruno longed to be on better terms with his father, and blamed his mother for the break-up. Doing an audit revealed these attitudes, and the reasons behind them.

It allowed Bruno to recognize he could love his father while not taking on board all his values and beliefs, and allowed them both to arrive at a compromise that would work for them. To his own astonishment, this not only involved Bruno getting behind Robyn going back to work after having a child, but him working from home so that he could take a share of the childcare.

DOING AN AUDIT

First, you need to fill each other in on some background. Go through the answers to these questions, and be prepared to tell stories and listen to reminiscences that come up because of them. While doing so, you may find some surprises. Your own history and family could hold some unexpected significances when matched with your partner's.

- ▶ Where were you born and when?
- ▶ Do you have siblings and if so how many?
- ▶ Where did you come in the family (that is, were you youngest, oldest, middle?)
- ▶ What was the gender spread (were you the younger sister of two brothers, middle of three sisters, etc.?)
- ▶ Did your birth family stay together or were your parents separated?
- ▶ If your parents separated did you still see both parents?
- ▶ Were you in care, fostered, adopted?
- ▶ Did you have step-parents?
- ▶ Did you have stepsiblings and/or half siblings?
- ▶ Did you move home while you were a child?
- ▶ Did your family go on holidays when you were a child – if so, where, and who went?
- ▶ Were your grandparents alive while you were young – did you have contact with them?
- ▶ Who else related to you did you have contact with?
- ▶ Did anyone close to you suffer serious illness while you were growing up, or die?
- ▶ Did you have pets in your family? What sort and what were your responsibilities with them?
- ▶ Were you expected to do chores in the home while growing up?
- ▶ Did you have a weekend or evening job while you were at school?
- ▶ What qualifications or training did you get?

- ▶ How did your family celebrate festivals such as Christmas and Easter, Chanukah and Passover, Diwali, Eid?
- ▶ What was the best and the worst thing that happened to you while you were growing up?
- ▶ When and how did you leave home?

What did you expect from your relationship?
We all have expectations. Look at these statements and each, separately, grade them.

	Disagree strongly	Disagree	Not sure	Agree	Agree strongly
I'm basically happy with our relationship					
I sometimes wish it could be the way it was when we first met					
I'm sure other couples are happier than we are					
Nothing will change the way we are together					
We don't need anyone else					
I'd never be attracted to anyone else					
My partner only has eyes for me					

	Disagree strongly	Disagree	Not sure	Agree	Agree strongly
All you need is love and that sorts out any problems					
A good relationship comes naturally					
Marriage makes any relationship happier					
Having children makes any relationship happier					
Having more money makes any relationship happier					
Having a nicer, bigger house makes any relationship happier					

What do you feel for your partner?

We sometimes put up with behaviour in a partner we'd never accept from a friend. So should we be applying the same standards to our partners as we might to friends? We may love them – but do we like them? And what do we mean by that?

	Disagree strongly	Disagree	Not sure	Agree	Agree strongly
There is nothing I want to change in my partner					
I like my partner's character					
I always thought my partner would change when we got together					
There are things about my partner I hoped I might change					
My partner has changed in the time we've known each other					
My partner often does things to please me or make me happy					

	Disagree strongly	Disagree	Not sure	Agree	Agree strongly
My partner often does things that upset, annoy or scare me					
My partner is different with other people					

Do you communicate?

Communication is more than an exchange of information – when you're getting home tonight, or instructions – turn on the washing machine! It's about building bonds and staying in touch by sharing feelings and thoughts. How do you do?

	Disagree strongly	Disagree	Not sure	Agree	Agree strongly
I tell my partner about my feelings					
I tell my partner what I think					
My partner tells me what they feel					
My partner tells me what they think					

	Disagree strongly	Disagree	Not sure	Agree	Agree strongly
We discuss our feelings					
I feel close to my partner					
We don't talk a lot but I'm sure we just know what the other is thinking					
I listen when my partner talks to me					
My partner listens to me					
I sometimes feel my partner doesn't listen to me					
I can tell my partner anything					
There are things I don't share with my partner					
I feel my partner keeps some things from me					

	Disagree strongly	Disagree	Not sure	Agree	Agree strongly
Everyone should have some secrets					
Least said, soonest mended					
I feel comfortable talking and listening to my partner					
My partner interrupts when I try to talk					
I think I don't always give my full attention when my partner talks to me					
My partner can do and say things that surprise me					
When my partner is unhappy I usually know why					

	Disagree strongly	Disagree	Not sure	Agree	Agree strongly
When I'm unhappy I can tell my partner why					
There are certain subjects we avoid					

Arguments

We all have conflicts – the issue is not that we argue but how we settle it.

	Disagree strongly	Disagree	Not sure	Agree	Agree strongly
We don't argue					
I avoid certain things in case it leads to conflict					
We often disagree but nothing changes					
We disagree but we find ways of talking it over and coming to a solution					
We have disagreements but respect each other's position					

	Disagree strongly	Disagree	Not sure	Agree	Agree strongly
When we disagree I know I'm right					
We have the same argument time after time					
When we disagree we can usually talk and come to an understanding					
When we argue one of us always comes out on top					
I can feel scared of my partner's reactions to disagreements					
I hate raised voices					
When we disagree it always ends in a fight					
I find it hard to apologize					
My partner can't take criticism or accept blame					

	Disagree strongly	Disagree	Not sure	Agree	Agree strongly
I find it hard to take criticism or accept blame					
When we argue it blows up into a fight but then we come to an agreement and it's over					
When we argue it simmers on for ages and never comes to an agreement					
When we argue one of us blows up and then feels better while the other goes on feeling bad					

Money

Money is often at the root of many arguments and difficulties for couples. How do you manage money between you?

	Disagree strongly	Disagree	Not sure	Agree	Agree strongly
I know what my partner earns					
My partner knows what I earn					

	Disagree strongly	Disagree	Not sure	Agree	Agree strongly
I don't always tell my partner the real cost of something I buy					
We both do household shopping so know the cost of what we need					
We argue about money					
When bills come in we talk them over so know how much we're spending					
I sometimes hide bills from my partner					
We have a shared account					
We plan our spending together					
We agree about what we spend our money on					

	Disagree strongly	*Disagree*	*Not sure*	*Agree*	*Agree strongly*
We spend more than we are earning					
Money is for spending not saving					
I worry about having enough to get by					
Men should earn more than women					

Leisure time

Do you have free time after work and all the things you need to do to run a home? Do you spend time together as a couple, and do you have time off from each other with friends?

	Disagree strongly	*Disagree*	*Not sure*	*Agree*	*Agree strongly*
We never have time to do anything together					
We never have time to see friends					
After my day all I want to do is collapse on the sofa					

	Disagree strongly	Disagree	Not sure	Agree	Agree strongly
I enjoy spending time with my partner					
I like seeing some friends on my own					
I don't like it when my partner has social time without me					
My partner doesn't like it when I have social time on my own					
We tend to agree on what we like to do together					
I'm happy to join my partner doing something I don't like but they do					
My partner is happy to join me doing something they don't like but I do					

	Disagree strongly	Disagree	Not sure	Agree	Agree strongly
We spend about the right time doing stuff together					
We spend about the right time doing stuff apart					

Sex

Sex may not be the be-all and end-all of a relationship, but managing it so both of you are happy about the sort of sex life you are having is important.

	Disagree strongly	Disagree	Not sure	Agree	Agree strongly
We have sex as often as I'd like					
We have sex as often as my partner would like					
We don't always agree on when we want to have sex					
When we have sex I enjoy it					
I always have an orgasm					

	Disagree strongly	Disagree	Not sure	Agree	Agree strongly
We talk about sex in a general way					
We talk about our sex life and our feelings					
I feel confident about my sexual knowledge					
I know what makes me feel good sexually					
I know what makes my partner feel good sexually					
You shouldn't have to ask a partner what does it for them, you should know					
I've been able to tell my partner what I like					

	Disagree strongly	Disagree	Not sure	Agree	Agree strongly
There are things I'd like to try but feel too shy or uncomfortable to ask					
There are things I'd like to discuss with my partner about our sex life but feel unable to do so					
I would never be unfaithful					
My partner would never be unfaithful					
If one of us were unfaithful we would still stay together					

Families and friends

How well do you and your partner get on with the people attached to them?

	Disagree strongly	Disagree	Not sure	Agree	Agree strongly
I get on well with my own family					
I get on well with my partner's family					
Family are important to me					
I have good friends					
I like my partner's friends					
We have friends in common					
Friends are important to me					
The amount of time we spend seeing family and friends is about right					
I wish I had more friends					
I wish I had different friends					

Doing what needs doing

	Disagree strongly	Disagree	Not sure	Agree	Agree strongly
We talk about big decisions and make them together					
We've talked about chores and share them equally					
Sometimes we argue about who does what					
I often feel I have to do too much					
It doesn't matter who makes more money between us					
We've talked about work and childcare and agreed how we'll manage					
Housework is mainly a woman's responsibility					

Children

Having children and bringing up children is probably the one thing that will most change your life. Have you talked about your feelings, intentions, wishes and fears about the subject?

	Disagree strongly	Disagree	Not sure	Agree	Agree strongly
We have talked about having children					
I know how many children I want and when					
I know how many children my partner wants and when					
We have the same ideas on when to have children and how many					
We have the same ideas on how to bring up children					
We have the same ideas on discipline and smacking					
Mums and dads are equally important to children					

	Disagree strongly	Disagree	Not sure	Agree	Agree strongly
We've talked about childcare responsibilities					
A relationship is completed by children					
Having a child with someone shows how much you love them					
You can feel the same about a stepchild as you do your own children					

Values and beliefs

	Disagree strongly	Disagree	Not sure	Agree	Agree strongly
We have the same beliefs about religion					
We agree on what's right and wrong					
Sometimes I think certain things are OK when my partner doesn't					

	Disagree strongly	Disagree	Not sure	Agree	Agree strongly
We agree on political beliefs					
Sometimes we disagree on our views about society					
I would never tell a lie, not even a white one					
I think I have a strong moral code					

The importance of a good and happy relationship

We've already mentioned the importance of happiness – to your mental and physical health, to your life chances and your family, friends and community. The bedrock of your happiness is often your relationship – how strong it is and how much it supports and enhances you. Having a good, strong, loving and caring relationship is the most important aspect of a happy family. However much you love your children and value being a parent, unless you and your partner are happy together there will be something missing. And however much you function well as parents together, one day you will be back as you were, a couple again. Unless the two of you maintain your own relationship – keep it vital, communicative, caring and sharing – during the years you bring up your family, you may one day wake up to find your kids are gone and so too is the relationship you once had. So it's really important while you are still a couple to put in place mechanisms for you to continue as a couple even when you have children to look after – to go on seeing each other as individuals, not Mum and Dad, to spend time alone together as lovers and best friends as well as a family, to put each other first even when you feel kids come first.

Exercise

Sit down with your partner and together think of three things you used to do as a couple when you first got together. Discuss:

▸ What you enjoyed about them.
▸ Do you still do them?
▸ If not, why not?
▸ Are there any things you don't do you'd like to do?
▸ Why don't you?
▸ What can you change now to help yourselves doing these or other things together.

Agree a time, once a week, when you'll make a date to pursue one old or one new experience.

KEY POINTS

1 If you share your life with somebody, your shared happiness is at the root of your individual contentment.

2 Our wellbeing depends on our fostering and supporting the wellbeing of those closest to us.

3 Happiness is positively good for you and passing it on sets up the 'ripple effect' that widens this pool of happiness.

4 It helps to learn about and understand the process of falling in love.

5 We carry a 'blueprint' and an unconscious 'checklist' of our ideal partner.

6 Birth order can be a powerful influence on choosing a partner. So too can childhood experiences provoking the urge to 'rewrite the script' of your life.

7 You don't have to be perfect or to pursue perfection. Getting your priorities right will be more helpful in finding you the best relationship.

8 You cannot really change another person but you can change yourself.

9 Auditing your relationship occasionally – 'Is this working, are we happy, shall we make any changes?' – is a good way of keeping it healthy and happy, or improving things.

10 Having a real and happy relationship can be the most important aspect of your life. It should be there for the duration – still there when any family has left, when you have retired or when you have simply grown old together.

BEING HAPPY

Sometimes we're so busy, so intent on all the things we have to do or think we should do that we forget to simply kick back, have fun and do the things that make us happy. So here's an idea: make a 'fun sheet'. Get a sheet of paper, stick it to your fridge door and every time you think of something that lights up your day, anything that cheers you up, activities you like to do or used to do and miss doing, or would like to try out, write them on the sheet. Have Small Things easy to do, Medium Things that take some time and effort, and Big Things you really have to save up or plan for. Make a point, every day, to do a Small Thing. Once a week, at least, do a Medium Thing. And at least once a month do a Big Thing. Every time you do one give yourself a gold star. You should each have at least 30 gold stars every calendar month and if you don't, sit yourself down with your partner and discuss why not.

Here's some ideas to start you off – what can you add?

Small things	Medium things	Big things
Watch a favourite programme. Read a book/magazine. Have a relaxing bath. Sit on a park bench and watch the world go by. Get a new app for your phone. Tell a silly joke.	Go to the cinema. Go out for a cup of coffee with a friend. Go for a walk. Download a new music track or film. Have a fantasy about a no-expenses-spared holiday.	Buy a new outfit (charity shop clothes are fine!). Throw a party. Go to a wedding. Plan a realistic holiday. Go for a spa day.

....

Baby makes three

In this chapter you will learn:
- *How attachment works and why it's so important*
- *About 'wearing your baby'*
- *About tackling crying*
- *About dealing with jealousy in adults and children*

And baby makes three

Having a baby can be one of the happiest experiences of your life. It can put the cherry on the cake of your relationship and really feel like a tangible bond between you, for now and forever. But the arrival of a child, whether first or subsequent, can also be the time when a wedge is driven between even the most loving couple and cracks can show in even the strongest relationship. To make this addition to your family a happy one, and the best present you can give each other, you do need to work together as a strong and loving unit and to be aware of how both of you, separately and together, might be affected by the situation, and what you can do to make it a positive step.

IT'S AN ART, NOT A SCIENCE

Parenting is an art, not a science. There's plenty that science can tell us that helps, which is why books such as this do offer support and sometimes a lifeline. If nothing else they tell you the concerns you may have are shared by many other parents – that's a relief! And, using what many studies and observations have shown, writers such as myself hope to give you some tips and tricks, some techniques and skills, to make your parenting that much more comfortable.

What I hope to do above all is make it happy. But it being an art means you can, and do, bring your own approach to the experience. And while science might be able to tell you want is probably going on and why, the art is that *you* are the best expert on yourself, your child and your family.

The most important thing to keep in mind is that when you begin, you are a beginner. Instinct and common sense may come to your aid but the reality is many new parents feel at sea and at a loss in the first few hours, days or even months. And actually, can definitely feel as if they are making it up as they go along for the next 18 years and beyond! That's neither unusual nor an indication you're doing it wrong. In what other area of life do we expect people to step in to a complex job with little experience and training?

Insight

My daughter-in-law told me when their baby was a few days' old my stepson Alex turned to her in panic saying 'Help! I don't know what to do here!' for her to reply 'Alex, I'm a beginner too – I don't know!' It was the best thing that could have happened because both of them then recognized they were in this together, starting from the same point but willing to ask for help and learn. They are outstanding parents and their daughter a very happy little girl.

COMES WITHOUT INSTRUCTIONS

You may have had a few months' warning, but when that baby is put into your arms you are catapulted, often it feels with little real warning and not enough (if any) tuition, into the first day of a new job. You may have read books and leaflets, have talked it over with your partner, family and friends, but you never feel quite prepared enough. And unlike just about every other new item in your life, this one basically does not come with instructions.

YOUR FEELINGS

So how do you set out to have a happy baby, in a happy family? You start off perhaps by dealing with the feelings both of you might have about the new arrival.

Babies change your life. It's no good insisting you'll be the same after you
have a child. You won't, your partner won't and your relationship won't.
That doesn't mean it will be any the worse. Or, automatically, any the better.
A baby cannot, simply by existing, make a shaky relationship stronger or an
uncommitted partner love you. What it will do is move a person into your
life, into your heart and into your living space.

One of the reasons it's so important to get your couple relationship
onto a firm footing before you start a family is that having a baby
so totally takes over your life. If you moved another adult into your
house it would affect your relationship. You'd have to deal with
their presence, their demands, their dirty socks. But having another
adult there is nowhere near as intrusive and overwhelming as having
a baby.

A third person in your relationship

Two people form an alliance. They may have moments of being fed
up with each other or totally in synch with each other, and all shades
in-between. But there is only the two of you. Add a third and all of
a sudden you have shifting alliances and jealousies. Three against
the world too often becomes two against the other – and which
two can alter from hour to hour. When we have a baby, we mostly
don't think of it in terms of inviting a new person to share our lives.
We see them as part of ourselves, which of course they are. But
they are also an entirely new individual, with their own needs and
demands. And parents can find themselves or their partner feeling
allied to someone other than their partner, and thus one or both of
them feeling rejected and left out. Parents often describe the first
days of a new baby as being like falling in love – being consumed
with emotion towards this new arrival, to the detriment of any other
involvement.

This means that both partners can feel left out of the sometimes
intense love affair going on between the baby and the other parent.
New mothers can feel that their partner no longer sexually desires
them, sees them only as a mother, and is lavishing their attention and
affection on the new baby alone. New fathers can feel really left out,

as not only mothers huddle protectively over the cot but all other family members and visitors do too. The couple need to call on all the work they might have done to make their couple relationship strong, vital and happy, to make this a circle of three, rather than a competing couple of alliances of two.

PARENTS TOGETHER

Babies – and toddlers, and children, and teenagers – really, REALLY, need fathers. Fathers can be an important part of their children's lives even if they live apart from them or, because of work commitments, have to spend long periods away. But the key to a happy child is the strong presence of a father as well as a mother in their lives. Yes, single parents and gay parents can do a terrific job and this in no way denigrates them. But – and I hate to say this since once I didn't believe it – the different genders while able to do everything the other does, do bring something different to parenting, and children benefit from that difference. But most important, if there is a father who is physically or emotionally missing children feel rejected, neglected, judged and found wanting. They blame themselves for the fact dad isn't there and feel it was their lack of worth that made it happen.

MUM, DAD AND BABY

Most fathers desperately, deeply, want to be good dads and do their best. They begin with the desire but often this wish is frustrated. It's extraordinary but there are still publications and professionals who seem to believe it's Mum and Baby rather than Mum, Dad and Baby. Some health professionals will direct all their attention to the female parent, ignoring the male parent – if he is there, because the assumption often is that he won't be, and it's hardly surprising that this can be enough to put some men off. Friends and families will often behave as if the child is the mother's only, gathering round and congratulating or offering advice and help to her, excluding the father. And all too often, when a man tries to gain the skills of parenting and be a part of it, he may be discouraged. Babies cry and new parents need to learn how to manage, and to develop their understanding and the baby's confidence, but if every time it happens a friend or family member swoops down, cries 'I'll do that!' or 'Now look what you've done' the hapless father can quickly decide he's incompetent and incapable.

WHAT CAN YOU DO?

▶ Before the baby arrives, make sure you have a tried and tested habit of spending time together as a couple.

▶ When baby arrives, you will have to put going out as a couple together on the backburner for a time, but make a promise to revive it as soon as you can, once past the initial attachment building phase of your relationship with the new arrival.

▶ Continue having some time together, even if it means doing it in-between feeds and naps, and only a case of snatching a brief moment to make each other a cup of coffee or offer a foot rub.

▶ Resist all well-meaning efforts by friends and relatives to cast mother alone as being the parent. There's a dad involved too, and it's the two of you with baby, not mum and baby.

Baby makes four or more

Making sure the two of you are working in tandem and seeing yourself as happily part of this new enhanced unit also means thinking about the rest of your family if you already have children.

GETTING YOUR CHILDREN PREPARED

When new babies have older siblings what happens around the pregnancy, birth and introduction of the new arrival to them can either set the scene for co-operation – thus happiness – or full blown sibling rivalry and unhappiness.

If you have children and your partner is the first person you tell you're pregnant, make sure your children are the second. Recognize they may not be disposed to see this as good news. After all, would you be delighted if your partner came home and said, with every sign of delight and excitement, 'Guess what? I love you so much I've decided to have two of you! The new spouse arrives in a few months time – won't that be fun?' Your initial response is unlikely to be 'Oh wonderful! A friend to love and to share with! What larks we shall have!' It's far more likely to be 'That so-and-so goes nowhere near my Lego!'. So your first job is to accept and acknowledge your child's feelings – all of them. Excitement, anticipation, curiosity and interest. But also anxiety, jealousy and even rage.

COPING WITH STRONG EMOTIONS

Accepting that a child has these emotions doesn't make them any more real or lasting. Ignoring them makes them simmer underground and grow. Denying them leaves the child with a horrible sense of being wrong and unacceptable – this guilt could make them hate the baby even more but more significantly it rebounds on them, making them feel bad about themselves. Accepting that bad emotions don't mean a child is bad, but are natural, normal and common, means you can deal with them. Talking them through allows a child to manage them, and also results in the emotions not only becoming controllable but less. The key is to help them put negative emotions into words not actions. So you can tell them it's OK to say 'I wish the baby wasn't here'. You can then be reassuring, and answer 'I can see you wish the baby hadn't taken your place but you have a new place, and I love you the same'. Sometimes, simply acknowledging their feelings is enough so: 'I can hear you're angry about the baby being here.' Accepting emotions also doesn't mean we accept actions. 'Yes, you're upset the baby is here. No poking, prodding or pinching.'

During the pregnancy prepare your children by:

- ▶ Reading books with them about pregnancy, childbirth and babies, talking over what a baby might need and want, and telling stories about them when they were babies.
- ▶ Help your child 'own' the new event by asking them to help you collect toys, bedding, clothes for the new arrival. Some children may be happy to pass on their own discarded things. Others may become ferociously protective, claiming back toys and clothes they've grown out of. Don't tell them they're silly, they can't have a use for them now.
- ▶ Be patient and understanding as a child reverts to baby behaviour – they may see it as the only way to claim your attention now, since you're about to or have replaced them with a new model! Give them time and the chance to cherish baby things and soon enough they'll appear and hand the things over, in their own time and under their own control.
- ▶ Discuss names for your new baby. If the new name can be one you, your partner and your children have chosen together they will feel all the more involved.
- ▶ Ask your children to help pack your bag for hospital and make sure they know there's a photo of them included.

- ▶ If you can, take your child along to a hospital appointment so they can be part of the impending event.
- ▶ Always talk about the new baby as 'Your brother/sister' or 'Our baby' rather than 'My baby'.
- ▶ Ask at your local library or bookshop about relevant books – there are plenty of good ones about how siblings can get along. Read them – again and again. And let the books and reading time together give your child the chance to voice and explore any worries.
- ▶ Talk through with your child about how they're moving from being the baby of the family, or the older child with one little brother or sister, to having a newcomer. Be understanding if (or when – most do) they slip back into babyish behaviour and reassure them they'll always be your baby too. It's a delicate balance – children do like being told they are now the big brother or sister, but not at the expense of losing what they might have felt is a special place or a special relationship with you. So when you boost them by saying they will be the big child now, recognize they could also take that as a loss of status as well as a gain. Instead of comparing children – 'You're better than the baby, you can help me!' or giving them labels 'You're my Big Boy!' reinforce a child's sense of uniqueness and specialness to you.
- ▶ It will help you if big changes for your older children are accomplished by the time the baby arrives – toilet training, a move to a new bedroom, weaning. But trying to do this in a rush or with a sense of a clock ticking can apply pressure to your child and make it difficult for them. And of course if you've got it done fairly recently by the birth, the chances are a child may backslide, as a protest or a way of claiming the love and attention they feel they've lost to the baby. She cries and poops in her nappy? I'll cry and poop in my nappy! And any child of any age may become whiney and clingy when a new child is presented. So be prepared for more work and attention needed than you expected. Taking as much parental leave as possible plus some extra holiday time may be necessary so there are two of you there in the first days, which can be overwhelming.
- ▶ It can be tempting to take up relatives' offers to have older children to stay with them while you find your feet. The problem with that is that it can reinforce a child's feeling that they are being replaced – they can feel all the more resentful and rejected

when they do come home to find the house orbiting around the new baby and all the changes that have happened in their absence. It might be better to accept it's hard work and go straight in.

▶ Introduce baby to child as soon as possible. There are also two moments that might set the scene for your older child to remember. For a start, when mum comes home from hospital, if someone else holds the baby so she can go straight to the older child for a welcome home cuddle, that can mollify them. And if, as soon as possible, you can let the child hold the baby – maybe set them up sitting safely in an armchair of on the sofa, with you in attendance – they will feel like a protective older sibling rather than the jealous also-ran.

Insight
There is plenty of evidence that close contact with a newborn baby promotes a bond, whether with mother, father or siblings. Inhaling the baby's pheromones is said to do this so give older siblings that chance, by having them hold the baby and snuggle close.

▶ Trust your older child, with explanation, support and direction, to be able to hold and do simple things for the baby. That will make them feel protective and special. But don't put too much pressure and expectation on them. Jealousy is natural and normal. Being left alone with a baby may be too much temptation to show negative feelings in pinches and pokes. Protect not only your baby but your older child from letting such opportunity arise.

▶ Celebrate their entry into big siblinghood with a special present, and ask all your friends and relatives to remember the child as well as, or indeed instead of, the baby. Sometimes you have enough baby clothes – a toy for your older child would be the greatest help you can have.

▶ Understand and forgive 'bad' behaviour. Behaviour is the way we show our feelings so if a child acts up, it's because something is worrying them that they're trying to get across to us. Children may well react to a new baby by testing you – now you've got another, do you still want and love them? Help them put it into words – 'Are you upset about the new baby? Sounds to me as if you're angry. Come and talk to me and let's see if we can make it better.'

- ▶ Keep to routines. If all of a sudden their bedtime routine, breakfast routine, daytime routine is disrupted your older child is bound to feel unsettled. Use the help offered by friends and family and work together with your partner to make sure life goes on as it did before. You might feel it helps to let them off the hook for the moment. In fact, it's more likely to alarm and upset them.
- ▶ Make sure you and your partner, and friends and family, make time to be with your older child for quality time. Don't make it all about the baby – it obviously helps the relationship between siblings develop if you talk it over, and let them have shared time. But your older child also needs special time just focused on them – their needs, wishes and favourite things.

What do babies need?

Children need and thrive on unconditional love. In many senses, that's it. It's as simple, and a lot more complex, than that. What children need is a foundation of knowing they're alright, that you love them and are there for them. But part of that involves also being able to set boundaries and rules and sometimes making yourself very unpopular by causing them grief and frustration by not giving them what they want or letting them do what they want. Sometimes, as the adult and parent, you have to balance immediate contentment against their ultimate good. And sometimes you have to also balance what they might want or need against what someone else – another member of the family or indeed you – need and want.

BEGINNING AS YOU MEAN TO GO ON

It helps to get a least the mindset needed right from the start. There are plenty of skills you will need. There are plenty of skills that will come into play much later than this, but that at least start from here. You might, for instance, realize that teaching conversational skills is something that will be vital as your child grows, but what's the use of it now? In fact, children who have had parents who talk to them from the beginning tend to have far larger vocabularies later on than children who have not been spoken to from an early age. Of course you'll coo and much of it may not be intelligible apart from showing love and creating connection. The point is that sometimes we have to get into habits early to make them stick. Speaking to, reading to, communicating with our children can begin when they are in the womb – it's never too early. In common with so many skills, it's better started young and simply extended and refined as appropriate.

A newborn baby has so much to learn – as do their parents. And perhaps one way to look at them is that they may be inexperienced and appear to be blank sheets but, right from the start, they have personalities of their own. There will be some things you simply can't expect them to do, or be able to do, for some time – such as talk, walk, control their bowels. It might be mind-bendingly exasperating to have a baby fill a nappy mere minutes after being changed, but the child isn't doing it to get at you or show you up, no matter how much it might feel like that. However, what a child is trying to do, from the beginning, is learn how to communicate with you, recognize you and bond with you.

WHO'S IN CHARGE?

There's a balancing act parents need to perform if they and their children are going to be happy. One size does not fit all occasions. We have had fashions in parenting, over the centuries and over the last few decades. Once the rule was that children should be seen and not heard, that parents' needs were all that mattered and children did as they were told. In such a traditional view the watchword might have also been that sparing the rod spoiled the child, and that what a parent decided was best for them was also best for the child. In the last century, the pendulum swung so that smacking was seen to be barbaric – and ineffective – and children's needs and desires came to the fore. What seems to have happened now is that many parents have lost confidence and not only put what they might feel to be their children's needs first but entirely push their own to the back.

My suggestion is that you see parenting as a continuum and a process. In the first months you do have to be at your baby's beck and call, to help them build a secure bond and the deeply felt assurance that you will always be there for them. But as your child develops, it's to their advantage that they also gradually learn to wait their turn, and that they can't have everything they desire exactly when they want it.

Insight

Babies may need a quick if not instant response when distressed. Toddlers and children need to experience disappointment and frustration, and to see that you are the boss and the buck stops with you. Once they become teenagers, however, the game changes again. That's the stage when you may begin to give up the reins, to pass some responsibility to them, and to enter into the stage of compromise, negotiation and interdependence.

So how do you begin?

Babies need three things. They need to be nourished – to have the food they need, when they need it. They need to be comfortable and safe – to be warm and clean and kept from harm and discomfort. But most important of all, they need to be attached. You could call this love, but it's more, and more complex, than that (although love itself is a very complex thing!). Attachment is what happens when babies learn that the people who look after them will nurture them. That means feed them but also cuddle them, keep them warm and protect them. When a baby knows you are reliable, consistent and responsive, they attach to you.

MULTIPLE ATTACHMENTS

One misconception that needs to be challenged is the idea that attachment has to be to one, primary, caregiver and that this should be the mother. In fact, parenting is an equal opportunity job. There is simply nothing, apart from breast feeding, that one parent can do which the other can't, that one parent can't be as good at, as the other. And babies can manage attachment to a number of people – mum, dad, siblings, grandparents. What they need is for you to stick around and be there – several of you can all be responding to the baby's needs at the same time to help build up that all important attachment.

SECURE ATTACHMENT

We know that a child's and later an adult's ability to self-soothe and manage anxiety can be traced back to having been reliably soothed as an infant. Toddlers with a secure attachment to their parents are healthier, have fewer tantrums and develop a sense of right and wrong earlier. Children with a secure attachment to their parents are more co-operative with them and others, and have and manage friendships with peers better. They learn faster, have higher self-esteem and are more flexible and resilient under stress. So it seems that making sure you have a secure attachment with your baby is a 'no-brainer'. And we know how best to do it.

Parents sometimes fear that going all out to make a really strong baby/parent bond might result in a demanding child – a child who cannot be without constant attention or go to sleep by themselves. In fact, research shows that the more a child is encouraged to attach strongly in the early months of their life, the better able they are to move on to being able to cope for themselves later. What you are aiming for is to have your child gain the ability to 'self-soothe' – to learn that they can manage anxiety, look forward to your return or attention, and to know when to settle down and sleep. Leaving a baby to cry itself out, far from teaching the child it has to learn how to manage, actually floods the baby with harmful chemicals that damage their ability to cope. Babies who are left alone inappropriately learn that there is no-one there for them. They learn not to expect to be cared for. By not being shown care, sympathy and understanding, they may find it hard to learn how to feel those emotions for anyone else. And being flooded with those chemicals can actually damage the brain, making it difficult or even impossible for them to feel sympathy or empathy later on.

EMOTIONAL RESILIENCE

Attached babies, on the other hand, show a range of emotional resilience and skills. They tend to be healthier, to be calmer and have fewer tantrums, to show kindness to others and know when behaviour is unacceptable and have a good sense of right and wrong. Attached children play better with their peers, cope with stressful situations more easily than children where there were difficulties in bonding and once in school learn faster and have higher self-esteem.

Of course, building attachments is hard work at first. It might mean you need to be not just on call for 24 hours but in close touch. Practising what we can call Attachment Parenting has consequences for you and those around you. It means, for a period, putting your baby first and structuring your life and your other relationships around this.

SHARING CHORES AND LETTING THINGS GO

It might mean the house gets messier and meals are delayed or simple. You and your partner, and any older children, will have to agree on sharing chores and having advanced plans on who does what to get important things done while still maintaining contact with your child. Of course you can put your child down for a time, to get food prepared or go to the loo yourself. But if she cries, she needs to be held – it's as simple as that.

WEARING YOUR BABY

In many societies nobody blinks at the idea of a baby being carried around, in skin to skin or at least in body heat proximity, by a parent or carer just about all the time. In such societies children are hardly ever left in a cradle or seat, watching their parent buzz about at a distance. Instead, children are carried in arms or in slings. We can do this too, and it can result in a far happier child, which means a happier parent. Yes, it can be tiring and yes it can get in the way. You may need to take things slower and make allowances. But what are the advantages?

By being up close and personal you never need to suddenly realize your child is distressed or needs you. Not only might you find even a cranky baby calms down, the close connection is likely to head off dissatisfaction or anxiety. It appears to take more time – in fact, because children held all the time as babies tend to be calmer, more co-operative, and easier to parent it saves time in the long run. But since the early stage of this really close connection only lasts for the first six to nine months, if it means the house doesn't get cleaned properly, so what? You'll have more time to do that when your child is older, and more likely to have a child who helps and co-operates with you if you put the work into attaching now. As it is, you can get more done than you might imagine with a child slung about you – and your baby will be delighted to watch you do it, whether we're talking washing up or going round the supermarket.

Insight

The period when you are really working at building the bonds of attachment with your child is the time to call in favours from family and friends. That's when you ask for help – to be driven to the shops, to be given a hand around the home. Getting other people to support you frees you and your partner up to do what is most needed at this stage – to stay in contact with your baby. Carrying, cuddling, changing and bathing, feeding – all give you both the opportunities to sing to, talk to, and bond with your baby.

Building the foundation

As your baby grows their needs change. While it's essential and positive in the early days, remaining this connected would in the long run be damaging. You'd get frustrated, and frustration leads to resentment and stress. But the most important aspect is that once your child can move around on their own, they need you to loosen the reins so that they can begin exploring – not just the world, but their own abilities. One of the reasons it's so important to build that foundation of a sense of safety and security, a conviction that you will respond if they need you, is so that they can feel able to strike out on their own. Toddlers and children need you and need to know you're there. But once past the totally helpless stage of babyhood, they need to know you are there in order for them to feel able to go away. Staying connected and doing everything for them, gives way to allowing them to try to stand, and fall. To try to walk, and stumble. To hold a cup, and spill it. It also means beginning to hear the word 'No'. When a baby grabs your hair, you gently pry yourself loose. When a toddler swings a tiny fist at a sibling, or pulls the cat's tail, you stop them and make it clear this is not allowed.

There are two traps we can easily fall into during the transition between babyhood and toddlerdom. One is becoming overprotective parents, wanting to extend the close connection phase beyond the appropriate time, to keep our children safe. Picked up, cuddled, cocooned they won't come to harm we feel. But in fact, they will. Because a child who doesn't have the opportunity to learn how to walk on their own two feet and suffer the minor bumps in doing so never gets to manage themselves. Minor bumps now are so much more preferable to major injuries later, which are what often happen to children who have been kept, not from danger but from beginning to learn how to deal with danger. Over protection gives the child two messages. One is that the world is a horrible, dangerous, hideous place. The other message is that you can't learn to cope with such things – you'd better stay hidden behind your parents because you're never going to be able to cope with it. Overprotection undermines a child's confidence in themselves.

TAKING SECOND PLACE

The other trap is thinking that just as you have been so responsive to your baby's needs, you must continue to be so – to put their desires and needs above everything else. But again, this isn't protective. If you've done your job and instilled in your child the belief that you will always be there when they really need you, you can now begin the second and equally important phase – telling your child that they are not the centre of the world, and sometimes must wait or take second place or simply cannot have whatever it is they want. Children have to learn how to cope with disappointment, and with boundaries. We need, as parents, to start setting limits so they can understand them. Part of keeping them safe is protecting them from the fantasy that being denied what they want will engulf them with rage or distress. The strong feelings young children have are overwhelming, and they need us to help them manage them. But it doesn't help if we try to sidestep their confronting those feelings by giving in. We feel so strongly for our children and their distress can be awful to see. And when they get angry, we often so want not to be the object of their anger – to stay the loved one, and the friend. Being a parent sometimes means having to take the hit – to allow them to be upset and angry with us, if it's in their best interest for us to say no. Of course we need to understand and empathize with how upset they may feel. That doesn't mean we should give in. Instead of talking a child out of their negative feelings, sometimes the best we can do is say we can see how angry they are, understand how upset they may be...but the answer is still no. And that's that.

CRY OUT OR PICK UP?

If you accept the evidence about attachment, as I do, you see that letting a baby cry is not the best response. Some experts will say you should leave a child in this state to 'cry out' because eventually the child will 'self-soothe' – come to a point when they cry themselves to sleep, and that will teach them to cope by themselves at a later date. In fact, the evidence suggests leaving a baby to cry simply floods them with stressful hormones. That doesn't help them stop crying or go to sleep. They eventually wear themselves into exhaustion and drop off, of course. But the flooding with stressful hormones physically damages them after a time – it holds back or even prevents some of their development. A baby who learns not to cry by being left is learning that no matter what their distress, no-one will come. They learn they've been abandoned and there's no point in looking for relief. Self-soothing is for later, built on a foundation of parental soothing now.

WHAT CAN YOU DO WITH A CRYING BABY?

We often say babies who cry, all the time or regularly at certain times in the day, are colicky. This is actually more of a description than a diagnosis since we're not certain why some babies suffer from colic and others do not. But it's not unusual. Colic is defined as a baby who cries for at least three hours a day, at least three times a week. That apparently describes 1 in 5 babies in the western world.

Check their diet

There are theories about diet, both the baby's if fed on formula and the mother's if the baby is breastfed. Some studies have suggested that breastfeeding mothers avoiding cow's milk and giving the baby some probiotic drops has an effect. Food allergies and a sensitivity to some formula or a gastrointestinal upset have all been blamed. The first thing you need to do if your baby cries a lot is discuss with your health visitor that you've checked they're healthy and that everyone who handles them has their techniques for changing, feeding and burping right. Are you all happy to jiggle the baby around, to sing and talk to them to soothe them, and to go on doing so as long as it takes?

Be patient

Whether you call it colic or not, if all the medical reasons have been ruled out, your baby is unlikely to go on crying like this for longer than three months. That may seem a lifetime at 2 a.m. when they've been wailing since early evening, but it is a beacon to hold on to. Keep telling yourself This Too Shall Pass...

Hold them

It's an interesting fact that colic seems to be a condition only found in societies that have lost the habit of holding their babies. In societies where babies are routinely slung around the body of a parent or sibling or grandparent all the time, they hardly ever cry and certainly not for long. We've got out of the habit in our society of carrying small babies, so maybe now is the time to get back to using a sling and get into the habit of 'wearing' your baby.

Insight

Love doesn't 'spoil' children. It doesn't make them demanding or selfish or arrogant. On the contrary, a child given plenty of love learns not only to accept it, and become secure and safe and confident in the knowledge of being accepted and acceptable, they also become good at giving love. When children develop secure attachments to their carers, their self-esteem and confidence, their ability to feel and show sympathy, experience empathy and demonstrate affection, all grow. And all of those increase a child's ability to learn and to develop.

Consider sleep arrangements

Some families, in the early months, have their baby to sleep with them. There are arguments for and against having your baby in your bed. Baby likes it, there is no doubt! But some babies are noisy or restless and you do have to balance up the comfort to the baby against whether it will stop you from getting the sleep you need, and how it impacts on you and your partner. Also, if you are going to do this, safety is an issue. Lying the child between you might feel better, keeping them away from any risk of falling out of bed, but if either of you are heavy sleepers there is a risk of your rolling towards your partner and squashing the baby between you. Having the baby on the mother's side means you can wake up when needed and breastfeed, while keeping them safe. But you do have to be aware of that drop, and either have the mattress on the floor for the period when your baby will share your bed, or push the bed against the wall, or have a bed wide enough for you to build a rampart with pillows and bedding to keep them in. If bed sharing is not your choice, have the cot in the room. A child's nursery or bedroom is a lovely idea – it tends to be the advertiser's shorthand code for a loving DIY dad, getting ready to welcome his new child. But young babies need to hear you breathe and you need to hear them. Certainly, SIDS or Sudden Infant Death Syndrome, also known as cot death, is less likely in a baby that sleeps in the same room as their parents but in their own cot for the first six months. Some parents move their baby into their own room in a matter of weeks, or months or even longer. That has to be a decision you take, judging when is best for all of you. You may want to be flexible. When you think the time is right, you can either put your baby to bed in their own room, or in yours, and then move the cot with a sleeping child in it to the other room. Some children take to it immediately. Some may need some practice runs.

Share

If it sounds as if I'm saying mum has to do all of this, let's stop that idea right now. A baby needs to be in close contact and preferably carried by people they know. That means dads too. When dad is around, it's really important that he has as much opportunity to have contact as possible. Not just holding the baby on his lap, not just rolling on the floor or the sofa and exchanging raspberries and other sounds. Carrying. If the baby cries it's not because he's doing anything wrong, because 'men can't manage'. It's either because this is a baby who's crying at the moment, and will cry whoever picks them up. Or because dad hasn't yet got the knack and the bond – and the only way he's going to get them is to practise.

Think about what's around them

One suggestion for why babies cry is that they emerge from nine months of comfort and are suddenly thrown into a world of cold draughts, strange sounds and no movement. They've heard their mother's heartbeat all that time, been suspended and rocked in a warm bath in the dark. Their brains need some time to get used to all that extra stimulation, and in the meantime they may cry as a protest, or cry as a way of releasing the tension such a shock produces. Some babies do this from the beginning, and others start after a few weeks. That may be because as they grow they become more aware of what's around them, and stay awake longer so getting more tired. You can do much to make the conditions more similar to the ones they've been used to. Some babies respond to 'swaddling' – being wrapped up in a blanket or fleece. Dimming the lights, singing or humming or putting on music with a beat that is the same as your heartbeat, can help. Some mums report putting on the washing machine or vacuum cleaner has the same effect. But most of all, hold them and rock them.

Don't take it personally

It's so easy to feel got at, as if your baby is judging you and telling you you've failed. Or to blame yourself for not being skilful enough to know how to help. The reality is that some babies cry a lot, and all babies cry to some extent and at some times. It's not your fault they do so, nor a lack of any effort or skill on your part if they don't stop when you do everything you can think of to help. Sometimes, you just have to wait until the distress stops or the crying has the effect the baby is after – to release that tension. Keep telling yourself 'Sometimes, babies have to cry…'

Relax

Babies can sense your emotions, which you can't help but show through your body. If you're happy your body is relaxed and loose. If you're under tension, your body will be tight and tense. If you hold them while feeling miserable, they will respond by crying. If you're on your own that may be the time to lay your baby down, make sure they are safe and walk away for a short time. But not to let them cry out – to let yourself calm down until you can go back. You don't want a vicious circle to be established where the baby cries and you put them down...so they cry, and you find it hard to hold them. Holding helps. Sometimes you may not believe it, but it does. The aim is to get back to it as soon as you can. One suggestion is to put on some music, with the joint aim of soothing the baby and yourself, but also making their cries less distressing to you. Wearing ear phones or buds can be a great help, until you or your baby has calmed down.

Sing

Babies like noise – it mimics the shush of blood and thump of heartbeat they could hear while in the womb. It really doesn't matter if you think you sound like a foghorn; your baby is not going to be holding up scorecards. Sing, hum, burble away. Making rhythmic shushing noises works as well. Tell them stories, talk about your day or what you're going to do, even though it will be months before the words have any meaning. As long as it's got a rhythm and comes from you, your baby will love it.

Feed them

Food soothes, whether from breast or bottle. It is worth noting that babies fed on schedule rather than on demand seem to suffer more from colic. Maybe that's because babies fed on demand are given what they want and need, when they want or need it. Breast is best, there is no doubt, from both a nutritional standpoint and an emotional one – there's nothing quite as soothing for a child as to be fed while being skin to skin with mother. But the one advantage of bottle feeding, which cannot be denied, is that it does give dad an opportunity to share. It means you can agree to dividing up night-time feeds, so both of you get a chance to sleep. Of course, if you are breastfeeding you can discuss with your health visitor about expressing milk for just that purpose.

....

Insight

Some parents worry that attending to their every need and being so responsive to a small child will stop them developing the ability to manage for themselves. Will it make them too dependent on you and stifle their ability to strengthen those muscles and crawl and walk away from you? On the contrary, since carrying or wearing a baby is for while they are helpless and dependent on you it builds up what is important at the time – their trust and confidence in you. Once a child gets to the stage when they want to begin to develop independence, you'll know because they'll let you know.

....

WON'T A BABY GET TOO USED TO BEING THE CENTRE OF ATTENTION?

Babies, and toddlers and children later, do think they are the centre of the universe. It's part of our job as parents to slowly disabuse them of that fantasy and teach them to be sympathetic and empathetic to others, and share the limelight. But we do this on the foundation of first giving them all the sympathy and empathy they will learn from us to apply to others. We need to sympathize with their fears, and empathize with their needs before we can expect them to turn it outwards. So yes, they do have to be the centre of attention, at first. And yes, that does mean we have to do a balancing act between them and their needs, and our own needs and those of everyone else in the family. Partners need to be aware of each other and make efforts to still make it clear they love and care for, and attend to and cherish each other, and any other children they have. Friends and more distant family members may have to be told you love them and care for them but don't have as much time for them at the moment as you'd like.

....

Insight

Babies will go to sleep when they are tired, if they are also well, well fed, comfortable and feel safe. Newborns tend to sleep around 16 to 18 hours a day – annoyingly, more during the day than at night. A child of any age is going to be scared of sleeping, and find it hard to drop off, if they're alone and insecure. Babies are sent to sleep by being rocked and held and soothed by your voice, not by being left to cry until they sleep from exhaustion. They tend to stay asleep if they can sense they are connected and secure, which is why they may well wake up and cry if you put them down.

....

CENTRE OF THE UNIVERSE

Babies are totally self-centred. That is, so to speak, their natural default and they can't be blamed for it. Indeed, when first born they don't actually know there is anything beyond them. They harbour the belief that they are the sun around which all else revolves. This is why babies and toddlers and children can indulge in 'magical thinking'. In other words 'My parents have broken up. It must be because I was bad, or didn't try well enough. It's my fault'. If you think you're the centre and the principle in your story, you also believe that everything that happens revolves around you and your actions. All children at some point experience anger or frustration. Children tend to believe theirs is all-powerful and all-consuming. A child having a tantrum is not only in the grip of an overwhelming emotion but also an overwhelming anxiety that their anger is dangerous and damaging. They can get flooded with emotion to the point of speechless hysteria, and at that point find it very hard indeed to calm down or think clearly. Being punished, being shouted at, being treated impatiently or asked to be reasonable can only make it worse because the child can't help feeling out of control, and terrified at what their feelings might do. We'll talk later about what you can do to deal with temper tantrums in toddlers, but for now it's worth recognizing that you start with a baby who thinks they are the centre of the universe, and you can't expect that child to believe any different. It's one of your jobs to quietly and lovingly help them see they're not, and as such not responsible for everything that happens around them, and to learn how to manage their feelings. It's about helping children see when things go wrong it's not their fault, but also helping them behave with sensitivity and empathy to those around them.

Think about the things that you enjoy – time with a partner as a couple, a cup of coffee with friends, a chance to relax with a magazine, a long bath or refreshing shower, a favourite TV programme, listening to music…

Write down as full a list as possible, then note for each:

▶ When do I do this?
▶ When was the last time I did this?
▶ How often do I do this?
▶ If not as often as I would like, what stops me?
▶ What could I do to make it easier to do this?

Use the last point to put in place an action plan to make sure you do take better care of yourself in future.

KEY POINTS

1 Baby makes three, but their demands can also divide the two. The best present you can give each other as new parents is to work together as a strong and loving unit.

2 Babies do not come with a set of instructions. You are a beginner and parenting is an art rather than a science.

3 Any problem you have as a parent has been, or is being, shared by many other parents.

4 Either partner can feel left out sometimes by the intense love affair going on between the baby and the other parent. You will need to work together to keep your relationship as a couple strong, vital and healthy.

5 Children of all ages really need fathers. Fathers are an important part of a child's life even if they live apart from the family or are kept away from it for long periods because of work or other commitments.

6 Children need careful preparation if three is to become four, or more.

7 Children need, and thrive, on unconditional love – it's as simple and as complex as that!

8 Right from their birth children need three things – to be fed, to be comfortable and safe and, most of all, to feel attached and that they belong.

9 Don't take things personally – your baby is not judging you – and try to relax. Babies can sense the emotions that you can't help but show through your body.

10 Babies see themselves as the centre of the universe. It is part of a parent's job, over the child's development, to gently and lovingly help them to see that while you adore and value them, sometimes they must come second.

BEING HAPPY

How are you doing with the fun sheet? Here are a few more ideas to add – do your own!

Small things	Medium things	Big things
Play games on Facebook. Blow raspberries on your baby's tummy. Be brought breakfast in bed by your partner. Finding money you'd forgotten in a coat pocket.	Have an inexpensive wine, lasagne and film night at home. An afternoon in the park or countryside, just sitting in the sun. Looking through photographs together.	Going away for the weekend to a family friendly place. Having friends who love babies come to visit. Going to the hairdresser when you haven't been for some time and really need it.

The toddler

In this chapter you will learn:
- *How to ACT not react*
- *About being an authoritative rather than an authoritarian or permissive parent*
- *About the importance of routines*
- *To deal with or fend off tantrums*

If being the parent of a baby is like the first days of a new job, having a toddler and then a child around is apprenticeship moving rapidly into degree course. Being a child is a process, as they move from helplessness and inexperience through practising and enjoying collecting skills towards self-sufficiency and independence. While much of how you handle your parenting may change over these years as you adjust to the differing demands and needs of a growing and developing child, the toddler years are the best time to lay the foundation of those skills. And, in effect, the skills remain the same – gain them now and they will stand you in good stead with an older child, a teenager or even a young adult. It's only the detail that changes, not the basics. The concepts are the same whether used with a preverbal toddler, a gradually maturing child or a stroppy teenager. Once you have the ideas and have honed the strategies on a preverbal toddler, you can also practise them on a child or teenager.

PUTTING OURSELVES IN THEIR SHOES

What's it like to be a toddler, and then a child? If we want to manage our family and make it as happy a place as possible we need to understand what is going on for our children. Once children start getting about on their own they become challenging. We may need to put ourselves in their shoes to make family life fun rather than one long confrontation. And having fun is a key concept. It's not just about being entertained or entertaining; the happier you are, the more effective a parent you are. The happier your children are, the more they are likely to be learning, co-operating, sharing, and thus the less stressed and the more effective you can be.

TAKING RISKS

Becoming mobile and gradually more self-sufficient is about taking risks and developing skills, about making needs heard and understood, and about listening too. Children can be defiant and demanding because they want to learn how to manipulate their own environment and can become frustrated and angry at the difficulties. Temper tantrums can be a feature of the so called Terrible Twos because it's the period when children want to make choices and manage for themselves but don't yet have the skills to do what they see those around them doing. This is a time to establish you will listen and explain. They may not yet have a full command of language but toddlers will be showing their discoveries and displaying a desire to learn and have their questions answered. Playing with and talking to children sends the message that they and their curiosity is acceptable. But this is the stage when you will need to put some boundaries in place. Boundaries tell children that they are not the centre of the universe, and that you are in charge. Children are naturally selfish and self-centred – that's how they are. It's our task to train them to be social and co-operative. Teaching polite behaviour helps our children become fit for their future.

'ACT' rather than react

Toddlers can be hard work and if you're going to enjoy being the parent of one – and you should – there is one vital strategy you need to acquire. This is knowing how to ACT rather than react.

In any interaction there are two influences – you and the other person. We often feel when children play up that the row is all about them and their behaviour – they're 'behaving badly' and they need to be sorted out.

In fact, what you bring to the interface is just as important – sometimes more so. If you come into a room already upset and angry because the milk is sour or you forgot to buy fish fingers and the first thing you see is a mess and a boisterous child in the middle of it, the situation can soon escalate into a row. You may shout at them for the disorder, they may not be able to see what is wrong or respond with cries or sulks, and soon you're at loggerheads. You may say the fault was the child's for leaving a mess; the child may simply not see the issue. You're both stuck. So it's important to be able to see that we need to recognize all sides of what is going on. A useful way of doing so is to remind ourselves to ACT not react. ACT stands for:

Adult

Child

Tools

A – the Adult's feelings and needs
Whenever you're in a situation that looks to be spiralling out of control, you need to stop and ask yourself 'What's going on for me? How am I feeling? What do I need to happen?'

You might initially answer 'Well, I'm annoyed at what this child has done. I need them to do what I want.' In other words, it was their fault for leaving a mess and you had every right to blow up at them. Is that the whole story? Could the whole answer not be 'I've had a bad day. I made some mistakes, things haven't gone the way I wanted, I'm tired and fed up and I felt ready to blow. I need my family to make my life easier. And I just needed a few minutes to calm down.' Your state of mind contributed to the eventual argument and the reality is that your child may well have been at the end of a long line of petty annoyances. You could call it 'kicking the cat' or letting off steam at one person because of your anger at other issues.

C – the Child's feelings and needs
Then, ask yourself 'What's going on for my child? How are they feeling? What do they need to happen?'

You might initially answer 'He knows I don't like him playing with all his toys in the living room. He just does it to annoy me and then won't listen to me when I tell him off.' Is that the whole story? Could the whole answer not be 'He was playing and is far too young to realize how I felt or what I wanted. Maybe if I'd been watching him or had him playing somewhere where it's OK, I wouldn't have been so angry. And he's tired and hungry – no wonder he cried and shouted.'

T – the Tools you have at your disposal
If you stopped and thought this through, you could then use the skills
you have – or will soon have – to find out how you and your child
could co-operate and fulfil both of your needs in this situation. In this
case, your need for some order, your child's need for a snack and a
bit of sympathy and both your needs for reassurance. The skills you
do have and will soon enhance are your toolkit – various tips and
strategies you have for managing your family as best you can. Add
that up: the Adult's feelings and needs; the Child's feelings and needs;
and the Tools you have. It spells ACT.

Insight
A very useful motto is: 'ACT, don't react'. Instead of reacting to your child's
behaviour at once, stop and think it through.

Acting instead of reacting can help in many ways. It encourages
you to recognize that what is happening in other areas of your
and your child's life and what they are actually capable, or not
capable, of doing can have an effect on what goes on between
you. It helps you see that how you behave has as much to do with
the situation as how they behave. It helps you to understand that
emotions about other issues can intrude in all sorts of places. And
it helps you begin to recognize that there are things you can do to
get control.

So always stop and think:

Adult: What's going on for me? How am I feeling? What do I need to
happen? Why?

Child: What's going on for my child? How are they feeling? What do
they need to happen? Why?

Tools: What can I say or do to help both of us get what we need?

What is the link between behaviour, feelings and needs?

Once you begin to think ACT you can see that childish 'bad
behaviour' is mostly nothing of the sort. It's actually the way that

toddlers, children and indeed teenagers try to tell us what it is they are feeling and needing. Bad behaviour is always about bad feelings, leaking out in action instead of words. The trick is to try and put a name to the feelings and then the needs, in order to understand why the child is behaving like that.

Behaviour, feelings and needs are a three-part puzzle. Think of it as three layers:

▶ The first, top layer is the behaviour – the obvious, visible piece of the puzzle. This might be, for instance, a child sitting in the corner demolishing the new toy just given them by grandma, with a black look on their face.
▶ The second layer is the feelings – which are perhaps hidden by the top layer. You may miss them because you're so focused on what the child is doing, being bad tempered and destructive. You may find yourself shouting at the child, taking the toy away from them and sending them off to their room in disgrace.
▶ The third layer is the needs – often completely obscured by the 'bad behaviour' but also by your frustration and anger at the child's behaviour.

The best way of imagining this behaviour/feelings/needs puzzle is to visualize it as a fountain. Above the fountain are the jets of water shooting into the sky and sparkling in the light. That's the first thing you see, that's behaviour. Behaviour can be laughing and dancing or shouting and crying – it's what you see and respond to.

But behaviour is driven by feelings, just as the fountains are driven by the water in the pipes. You can often tease out and recognize the feelings if you look hard enough – some of them will be hidden, like the water still in the pipes. Some will be evident, like the water just gushing out. In this case, the clue is in the fact that the toy was given by grandma as she rushed past to coo over the new baby, who then took up all her time and attention for the duration of the visit. Grandma has just gone, only briefly saying goodbye to her grandson, who she's hardly spoken to all the time. Perhaps if you sat down with the child and said 'Sounds to me as if you feel left out. Did you want grandma to play with you? Did you feel angry at the baby for taking up all her time?' He's not going to hurt the baby, he knows that's wrong. But he can take out his hurt, anger and jealousy – the feelings he's expressing – on the toy.

So you may pick up on the feelings being shown in the behaviour. What about the needs? The needs may be the layer you miss entirely, as it's hidden like a reservoir of water underground. But that reservoir drives the water in the pipes to create the fountains in the sky. That reservoir is what behaviour is all about. We often have to dive under the behaviour to try to understand not only the feelings but the needs – to listen to the tune not the words. Behaviour is the signal to look for feelings, which are what can help us work out the need.

In this case, it's to be noticed, to be appreciated, to be valued, to be loved as much as the new sibling. Powerful needs and all legitimate.

THE FEELINGS BEHIND THE BEHAVIOUR

Feelings are not right or wrong, they are just a normal part of being human. There is nothing wrong with feeling angry, jealous, frustrated or rejected. Sadly, we do sometimes judge people or blame them for what they are feeling. When a small child expresses jealousy for another sibling, we might try to control or banish what we see as something negative – or even destructive – by denying it 'Oh no, you don't mean that!' or making them feel bad for feeling that way 'What a horrible thing to say!' What the child hears is 'What a horrible little boy you are to feel like that!' They feel confused, because they can't control their feelings, so they start feeling bad about having them.

Feelings are not right or wrong, good or bad, they simply are. What matters is what we do about them. While making someone feel bad about feeling angry, jealous or frustrated might curtail the immediate behaviour which could be directed against someone else, it doesn't deal with either the underlying feelings or the needs adequately. When someone feels bad about having an emotion, it doesn't go away. Instead, the feeling might be directed against themselves, as they blame themselves for feeling that way. Or it might come out later, in more disguised or indirect ways: self-disgust, depression, eating disorders, self-harm. Either way, bad feelings emerge. And of course, denying or blaming themselves for their feelings doesn't deal with the underlying need. Understanding and accepting needs – both ours and other people's – cuts through blame and judgement and copes with them. Understanding the Behaviour, Feelings, Needs Fountain can often help us to dive underneath what appears to be careless, simply 'bad' behaviour and recognize our children are trying to say something, and it helps to listen.

Shared play

When they are babies we tend to know, instinctively, that our children need as much input as possible from us. They're helpless and receptive, so to learn about connection and loving, we need to hug and hold them and make plenty of eye contact. To help them learn things can go away and come back, we play peek-a-boo. To learn words, and walking, we talk to them and sing to them, and hold their hands and then let go. As they grow into toddlers and then children, our input develops and changes. Shared play is vital – we still need to join them in building with blocks and Lego, in learning and enjoying board games and jigsaws and using dolls and figures in imaginative play, where the child invents the story of what is happening to their toys. Above all, we need to read to them as well as gradually coach and encourage them to read for themselves. But the parents of a toddler and child need to gradually draw back. Of course you may still need to demonstrate but more and more often your child needs you to guide rather than take over. It's often really hard. Our own childhood may have been one where parents were prone to push forward saying 'Let me do that for you', 'You're doing it wrong – let me' or 'You're so slow – I'll do that for you.' It's easy to repeat that if it happened to you, but we need to hold back.

RESPECT THE STRUGGLE

Respecting the struggle is a technique that can help at any stage of a child's life, but starts here. Of course you wouldn't stand back and let your child walk into the path of a car or stick their fingers in a power socket so they can learn for themselves. But there are plenty of occasions when we have the temptation to leap in and do it for them, or help them, when in fact it would do no harm to let them try. For instance, when a child wants to carry a full cup across the kitchen, or use building blocks on their own. When they don't do it well or don't manage first time, instead of telling them off and cleaning up, or showing them how to do it, it's far more effective and a much better opportunity for both of you, if you say 'Well, that's hard isn't it? Shall we try it again?' Instead of taking the cup from her, make sure it's full of water that doesn't stain, and cold so it doesn't burn. And then, what does it matter if it spills? Hand the child a cloth to clear up and try again. Your job is to make sure the accident is as pain free and damage free as possible. The child's job is to try and try until they get it right. They can't get it right if you intervene.

We also need to let children do it for themselves. Children thrive best when encouraged in independent play. This means biting a lip and holding back a hand when they struggle to do something. Of course we can do it so much more competently and quickly. And maybe we feel if we show them how they'll learn more easily. In fact, the more often we 'show them how' the less capable they may be, because what we're actually teaching is that we can do it while they can't, and that's discouraging. Children may become used to the idea that 'that's too difficult for me, so I won't even try.'

We call the two types of play directive and non-directive. Directive is when you tell them how, show them how, criticize when they make mistakes, tell them how easy it is, how silly and clumsy they are. Non-directive play is when you:

▶ Give the child attention and encourage them to do it for themselves.
▶ Allow the child to learn from their mistakes rather than 'showing them how to do it'.
▶ Accept they might do it differently from you.
▶ Acknowledge and respect their choices.
▶ Follow the child's lead and suggestions rather than jumping in with ideas.
▶ Develop a helpful, open attitude – noticing what the child is doing and describing it to them.
▶ Be 'in the present' and spend time focused on your child.

It's not easy! We're so used to being helpers and guides and it can be difficult to shut everything else out and focus on this sort of play, conversations or activities. With two or more children it can be very difficult. But even setting aside a very short amount of time to do it properly will be helpful. The trick is to seize the moment when your child comes to you and wants to do something, to be with them.

THE VALUE OF NON-DIRECTIVE PLAY

There are three important positive effects of non-directive play:

▶ It has far reaching and lasting positive effects on the child's self-esteem.
▶ It builds closeness and trust between you.
▶ It helps development and learning, now and throughout their childhood.

Trying it for yourself could persuade you of the very powerful value of supporting children in finding out for themselves – and help you see how unhelpful it can feel to be shown how to do it. Try this: spread a load of your child's toys or games on the floor and sit down amongst them with a friend or your partner. Toss a coin for who will go first as child and who will be adult. Then, whoever is the child, begin to play with your toys. Whoever is the adult should then take charge, telling the other what to do and how to do it, showing them the 'right' way, criticizing their ideas. Do this for 5 minutes. Swap over and play again for 5 minutes.

Then, discuss:

How did it feel as the child?

How did it feel as the adult?

What did 'the child' do when directed?

What was the result of the play session – peace and harmony or tension?

Then, try it again but this time with non-directive play.

Spread a load of your child's toys or games on the floor and sit down amongst them with a friend or your partner. Toss a coin for who will go first as child and who will be adult. Then, whoever is the child, begin to play with your toys. Whoever is the adult should sit back, giving a commentary on what the child is doing but neither telling them what to do or how to do it. Do this for 5 minutes. Swap over and play again for 5 minutes.

Then, discuss:

How did it feel as the child?

How did it feel as the adult?

What did the 'child' do when left to their own devices?

What was the result of the play session – peace and harmony or tension?

Essential points

▸ An important strategy is to learn to ACT not react
▸ Understanding the link between behaviour, feeling and needs is vital
▸ We need to Respect The Struggle, and encourage non-directive play

Transitions

The transition from being the parent of a baby to the parent of a toddler is challenging in all sorts of ways. On one level, it's an opportunity to ease off and get some of your life back. Having established strong attachments by remaining connected, by carrying your baby a lot, you can now put them down and let them crawl, then walk, then run. By no longer having to be so much at your baby's beck and call you may feel you can reconnect with your partner and other children. But of course, while you have your hands free you now have them full trying to keep your increasingly active toddler safe. Babies may need contact and carrying but they don't need control. Toddlers, it would seem, do.

WHEN THEY BEGIN TO TODDLE

But this is the point where all that hard work creating an attachment pays off. One of the most important skills you learn and deploy as children grow up is setting appropriate limits. And it's far easier setting appropriate limits if you have empathy with your child, and your child, thanks to your attachment to them, has the beginning of empathy themselves.

When a child starts to struggle into being a toddler you can 'over-parent'. By this I mean trying to control your child either by setting strict limits on them and forever reminding them – 'No darling, you can't do that', 'No darling you mustn't do that' or 'No darling let me do that for you' when a child wants to get down and walk for themselves, or tries to build a tower or carry a cup of water. In other words, you wrap them up in cotton wool and are constantly herding them. Being over protective has several effects. It undermines a child's trust in themselves. Of course they are struggling – this is all new and they're trying to learn the skills to manage. But they're never going to do it if you keep interrupting. And they'll soon lose confidence in their ability to learn and manage if you don't let them try, or tell them off or swoop in immediately to clear up when they fail.

THE IMPORTANCE OF LIMITS

But children do need limits. It's your job to set and maintain them, but at the same time respecting the child for wanting to push those limits. Trying to over-control an enthusiastic, curious, exploring toddler will result in an angry, rebellious, unco-operative child. Because the child knows perfectly well it's their job to learn and explore, and stopping them is curtailing their development. But it's your job to make that safe, while helping them to do it. Letting the child have free rein is just as emotionally damaging. And here's an interesting difference between baby and child. When a baby wants something – food, comfort and love, contact – and wails for it, that's because this is what they need. Children sometimes wail for, insist on, run towards things they most certainly do not need and shouldn't have – freedom to run into the road, to punch a sibling, to grab a toy, to spill a hot drink. Your task is to let them run and stumble when it helps them to learn, and to say no, when it helps them to learn. Limits are important, but they need to be the right ones.

THE AUTHORITARIAN PARENT

Being too strict – being, in other words, an authoritarian parent – stifles children. There is a fine line between being an authoritarian parent, and an authoritative one. Being authoritarian means being not only strict but rigid – having a set of rules and laying them down, no matter what. Being authoritative means seeing things from a child's point of view, having not just sympathy for them and their struggles but also empathy with their feelings, and adjusting your rules and responses to take all this into account. Being authoritative is 'child centred' – we do what we do because we know it is, in the long run, the best thing for the child and for everyone else in the family. It means being responsive to their needs and being guided by the child – recognizing and understanding what's going on for our child rather than always imposing our will on them – reserving the right to take over, of course, if safety and wellbeing demands it. And being child centred doesn't mean ignoring or denying our needs or over-indulging the child either: it's a balance. But it's about them, while being authoritarian tends to be about us – we do what we do because that's what we want.

Insight

Research has shown that children with the most challenging behaviour tend to get less child-centred attention, and that a key way of changing such behaviour is to increase the amount of child-centred attention There is a clear link between attention and behaviour and the reality is that disruptive behaviour is a way of getting attention – from the child's point of view a negative reaction such as being shouted at or hit is still preferable to no attention at all.

But what's wrong with putting your foot down and telling your children what's what? If we accept that limits are important doesn't that mean strict limits are the goal to aim for in parenting? What happens when we parent sternly?

I would say there are six drawbacks to too strict parenting.

It's based on fear and teaches might is right

If children only do what you want because otherwise you'll punish them how is that different from being pushed around by the playground bully?

It teaches insincerity

If you know someone will come down hard on you if you break the rules, and you feel some of the rules are unfair, the result is often that you become very good at breaking them behind people's backs.

It's ineffective – it tends to lead to rebellion

Children from authoritarian homes tend to rebel – either at home with their parents or later when they leave home. They may later follow much of their parent's model, in bringing up their own children with a firm hand – but neither they, nor their children, seem to enjoy it, and there is often an emotional gap between them and their parents.

Love and happiness tend to be in short supply

Children may have been told they are bad, and need to be punished and kept in check, rather than being helped to behave well, and to understand their impulses and manage them. Family life can then feel as if it's all about control and trying to be accepted, than about laughter, joy, love and happiness.

It doesn't give children the chance to learn to set limits for themselves

The best discipline is that which is 'internalized' – when children learn that behaving in certain ways is good and right and nice and kind because that way everyone benefits.

It's hard work!

Being an authoritarian parent is an uphill struggle, because children will always push against the boundaries and you will always feel you have to maintain them no matter what.

THE PERMISSIVE PARENT

But being permissive is almost as bad as being authoritarian, and just as harmful for children in the long run. A child may be delighted with a permissive parent who lets them run around as they see fit, getting what they demand and not doing what they don't want to do. In such families, it seems as if it's the child in charge with nervous, unconfident parents. Plenty of us do give in to our children at times, but not because we've calmly weighed it up and decided it's the best thing. We give in to our children's demands because:

▶ It seems easier – say yes or stop saying no and we can stop fighting over whatever it is we've allowed.
▶ It feels better – when a child is frustrated, their feelings of anger, pain, misery seem so unbearable that it hurts us. We say yes to save their feelings – but actually, to save our own.

It might seem – and some parents may argue strongly – that allowing a child free rein is letting their creativity and natural goodness out. Following on the arguments for non-directive play, you can make a case for encouraging children to follow their impulses in all sorts of ways. What's the difference?

We let them get away with things, and that hurts them.

It may be such a relief to give in to a child's demand to have another biscuit, to avoid brushing their hair or teeth, to stay up one more hour. The arguments stop for a time. But, you have a tired child next morning, hair becomes even more tangled and teeth can decay. In other words, your peace and quiet now is paid for by your child suffering harm in the long run.

They never learn to manage disappointment

Kids need to learn that no means no, and if that means you're unhappy, tough. Disappointment, while unpleasant, isn't going to kill either of you. As parents there is a temptation to feel it's your job to fix everything – to not let your child suffer, ever. By trying to protect them from any pain you do several not very helpful things. You tell them that frustration and discomfort are absolutely terrible, intolerable things to have to endure and not only will you do everything possible to help them never to have to contend with them so must they.

They never learn boundaries

If you always give your child what they want when they want it how can they learn boundaries? The self-discipline to work for results or pace yourself, to share and make choices, are all based on a parent instilling discipline rather than a sense of self-entitlement. Children learn to push and manage themselves when you can tell them no, this far but no further, when appropriate.

They base their happiness on one more thing

Children will want this, want that and always ask for more. What is often behind this is a belief that your giving is a proof of love and attention. If you keep responding, they will continue to feel they are only validated or loved or even noticed if they can have one more thing. Instead of valuing love, communication and attention, they will fixate on things – another article of clothing, another piece of electronics.

We let them get away with things and that hurts everyone else

A child allowed to grab the last biscuit, or run around screaming in a cafe, means another child deprived of their fair share, or a cafe full of people having to endure your screaming child. But of course, that hurts your child too. They become the target of annoyed siblings, or glared at by total strangers. Worse, they learn they can get what they want if they scream loud enough and will continue to do that, through childhood, into teens and adulthood.

So what can we do?
To be an authoritative parent we have to:

▶ Take the hit.
▶ Bring in discipline.

Take the hit

Yes, it's not nice to have to be firm and not be Popular Parent for a few minutes. But that's the deal when you become a parent – you're the responsible adult and have to be grown up. The buck stops with you and it's your job to make decisions, and make them stick. We all need boundaries and limits, and if we're lucky we learn them from parents who are prepared to show us they love us, by saying no.

Bring in discipline

Discipline is a word that's much misused. It's often taken to mean punishment. We say discipline when we mean correcting a child, penalizing them in order to train and control, to correct or chastise. Particularly, we often mean to smack. But the word comes from the Latin for instruction or tuition. It really means to teach; disciple or pupil comes from the same word.

We bring discipline to our children by:

▶ Showing a good example.
  It's no good telling a child 'Do as I say, not as I do!' They won't. They will always follow your lead. Telling your child off for swearing or hitting and later for smoking or drinking will have not one jot of effect if you do any of these. Even if you think you only do them when your child is out of sight or hearing, don't fool yourself; children are better than secret police in finding out the truth.
▶ Protecting them.

If you don't want small children to break objects or put their fingers, hands or noses where they shouldn't (or, for that matter, put objects up their noses or down their throats) don't leave it to them. Put temptation out of reach and child proof your home until you are sure they can act in self-protection. Around the age of 21?

▶ Using positive discipline.

Children actively want to please us. That is, so to say, their default setting. Yes of course they can become defiant, demanding and self-centred, usually because making a stand and asserting their own needs and wants is part of their development. They can struggle and become frustrated and so act up, but it's not because they're bad or naughty, it's because they are learning and sometimes we all want to run before we can walk. But the bottom line is, however much they want to do things on their own or for themselves, however much they may want to do what they want rather than what you want, they want and need your approval, acceptance and love. This means you have an enormous advantage when it comes to teaching social behaviour and drawing boundaries; a child would rather you were happy with them than not. How can you use this?

HAVE A POSITIVE ATTITUDE

This book is about happiness, so that's the first and most important tip: look for happiness. Look for the fun side. If you spend all your time with your child struggling to assert control, force your child to do as you say, or behave exactly as you would like when you want, all both of you may feel in the end is exhausted and stressed. You've had no fun. And children can be such fun. So set out to see the upside, enjoy the positive bits and capitalize on the constructive elements. The more you look for and expect them, the more you'll see them.

POSITIVE PARENTING

This means setting out with the intention of:

▶ Noticing all the good things your child does, praising and thanking them for it.
▶ Ignoring minor whines and whinges, annoying or naughty behaviour.
▶ Choosing your battles.

Routines

Instil routines. Getting children to do as you'd like is so much easier when they have a routine to keep to. When it's a given that mornings mean getting up at a certain time, getting washed and dressed and sitting down to breakfast; or that evening meal is followed by bath time and story time and bed time, you're much less likely to have conflict over any of these.

INSTILLING ROUTINES

Children need the security of routines. When you think of all the really important aspects of a child's life – getting enough sleep, eating the right foods, being ready to move on in developmental stages – most of them are so much easier and more pleasant if we have a habit and a routine established to ease us all into it. One really vital aspect of a child's life is sleep – getting enough, going to bed happily and sleeping through. It will help if you see the importance of a routine, and it's a test case for how useful a routine can be.

BEDTIMES

Children need sleep. Because they sometimes can fight going to bed, and fight going to sleep, it's easy to forget that simple fact. But we all need sleep, to refresh and renew ourselves. If we or our children don't get enough it may not show in tiredness – so we may not make the link – but in crankiness, and impaired performance. We don't do so well in our work or in our relationships, and they don't do so well with you or siblings, in playgroup or at school. If there's conflict in your family and you're not as happy as you'd like, you and your family's sleep and sleep patterns may be something you need to address.

How much sleep?

Every child is an individual but as a rough guide, one-year-olds need 14½ to 16 ½ hours of sleep a day – naps morning and afternoon of one to three hours should be part of that; 2- to 3-year-olds need 10 to 12 hours a night and 1 to 2 hours' nap a day; 4- to 5-year-olds need the same night-time rest but may not need the daytime nap. Those aged 7 to 12 will need 9 to 10 ½ hours a night.

Children of this age are not only naturally active but developing very quickly. This means their minds are racing and their bodies are trying to keep up. It makes it hard to calm down and wind down at the end of the day. And you have quite a short window between their being alert and lively, and exhausted. Catch them in-between, when they are tired and ready for sleep, and bedtimes are relatively easy. Miss the window and they are overtired, cranky and frustrated, and you may then have a battle on your hands as they fight sleep even though they need it.

Bedtime routine
If you establish a bedtime routine it helps in so many ways. You have structure and a timetable – things children need and understand. The routine is calming, predictable and carries you from Point A (children up and around) to Point B (children safely asleep) seamlessly.

A bedtime routine starts well before bedtime. About an hour before you want them asleep, begin by supervising and encouraging them to clear away toys and board games, crayons and paint materials and by turning off TVs and any other electronic media. An exception might be music players – a CD of soothing music or sounds can help. But no flickering screens, of any sort. Television programmes, films, anything on the computer are counterproductive. Your children may like them and you may even think some are calming and restful. But anything on a screen is stimulating.

You may at this point want to prepare for the next day. If you're home with a small child you can do this on the day itself, but with a child at nursery or primary school it may help to do it in relative calm in the evening instead of in a hurry in the morning. Have your child choose clothes and lay them out, get some of a packed lunch ready, partly pack a bag and check if there is anything that needs to be remembered for playgroup or nursery. Later it may be materials for a lesson, letters to return, or special kit.

Then, head for the bathroom where children can bathe, brush hair and clean teeth. All are important in themselves but a bath, and the act of brushing hair, can promote peaceful feelings and behaviour. Lavender in the bath aids relaxation and conditioner after shampoo avoids tangles, and arguments over hair brushing.

Then you can either go straight to their bedroom or start in the living room. Whichever, the key is to choose quiet, calm, relaxing activities. With preverbal toddlers, sing lullabies, play quiet cuddling games, tell stories – even before they can understand, songs and stories are beguiling because they hear and relax to the sound of your voice. This will set the routine so that when they are older and can understand, you can read and tell stories, listen to music, chat about your day and plans for tomorrow. Finally, move to bed. Again, read and chat. When children are used to this as a routine, as they get older this will be the perfect time to talk over any concerns or worries or anxieties, share plans and ideas and funny ideas.

Anxiety

Overtiredness is one reason children may fight going to bed. Another is separation anxiety. By this we mean that children are scared – of being abandoned by their parents, or of abandoning them. They're frightened that once out of sight you may be spirited away. And another is actual separation. If children do not have enough time and enough connection with the people they love, their separation anxiety isn't a fantasy – it's real. They haven't seen enough of you in the day and so hate to miss you by going to bed. All the fears they express – of monsters under the bed, of bad dreams – and all the excuses – another drink of water, of being unable to go to sleep – come down to these.

Reading

Some parents hate reading to their children. They find it embarrassing and difficult or are worried books are expensive. They may opt not to have them, or to offer CDs of other people reading stories. But it cannot be too often and too loudly stressed: reading bedtime stories to your children is just about THE most important activity there is.

Why?

Partly, because it encourages the idea of reading being something you do and they can do, which encourages literacy which supports learning. But the other really important aspect of reading together is that it gives you the opportunity for a quiet, reflective time together. Children adore the chance to cuddle up with a parent in a one to one situation, for a safe period of time they know is theirs. Around the reading they can ask questions, not just about the content of the book but about you and them and life in general. Having bedtime story time gives children, as they grow up, the chance to confide and share all sorts of issues that worry them, frighten them or puzzle them.

Bedtime stories also give you a fund of references – little jokes and shared allusions – which you can bring up whenever you need to make them laugh or make them understand something, or simply say 'Here's a little bit of magic we have in common'.

And if there is any issue you want to put into words, whether the more serious areas such as a death or illness in the family, or where babies come from, or why the moon changes shape, there will be a book that helps by putting the dilemma in a safe and manageable form.

How?

Children really don't care how you read to them, only that you do. They're not going to criticize your reading skills. They may, on the twenty-seventh rendition of the story of a certain ravenous insect, pull you up if you get a word wrong or miss a sentence out. That's because they have been hanging on every word and can probably recite it word perfect themselves. But it's not a criticism of you. So embarrassment is so futile. This isn't being hauled up in front of class and humiliated. It's sharing something precious with someone who loves you. You don't have to do all the voices differently – although, as you gain confidence as you see how wonderfully your efforts are welcomed, you may be able to try. There's no judgement going on – just enjoyment.

When it's time for lights out, finish the story, kiss and hug and tuck them up. Have a goodnight 'sign off'. It could be 'Goodnight, sleep tight, hope the bedbugs don't bite' or 'Good night, sleep tight, and pleasant dreams to you. Make a wish, close your eyes, your sweet dreams will come true!' Or 'Here comes the flight to dreamland. Heads on pillows, eyes closed tight, don't miss the flight – good night!' or 'Goodnight stars, goodnight moon, go to sleep and wake up soon!' You can make up your own one for your family but the key is it's a magic spell – once said, that's goodnight.

DON'T GIVE IN!

Again, as with so many issues the really important thing to keep in mind is not to give in if you've set a rule or a routine. That's not to say ignore a truly distressed child. Nor that if it isn't working you might need to rethink and talk through what might be changed with someone who can support you and be objective, such as your health visitor, GP or at the family charity Family Lives. And of course routines and rules have to be adjusted as children grow. But standing firm is vital. When you give in to one more 'Perleeeeeeze?!' you train your children to know that all they have to do to get what they want is to wear you down and go on pushing. Every time you say 'Well, just this once...' you reinforce the idea that your rules are not rules and your boundaries can be breached. Set the standard, then keep to it.

Fussy eaters and fat children

Food and sleep are probably the two issues that most concern parents when their children are young, and they are linked. Children need good nutrition and good sleep to be able to grow up healthy and happy. Setting rules around mealtimes and bedtimes, and being confident in their necessity and their implementation, are vital so we need to understand why they are important and how we can apply them. When children can see parents enjoying different kinds of food (but using food neither as a comfort nor a bribe or punishment), and both preparing it and eating it, it teaches them about pleasure and permission to enjoy, and can be protective against food fads, weight worries and image problems which actually start as early as this time.

> ### Insight: Sitting at the table
>
> Most UK highchairs share the design that gives the child a built-in table. The child may be eating at the same time as everyone else around your table, but is off to the side and excluded. Rather than encouraging small children right from the beginning to feel part of eating with the family, it separates them and almost forces you to feed your young child alone and cut off from the family gathering. In contrast, many Scandinavian designs offer a high chair with an adjustable seat and footrest, cushions and harness and restraining bar, but no table. The idea is that the chair is pulled up to the table so the child shares with everyone else and is part of the fun. They seem expensive but because they are adjustable can last their entire childhood, and set a tone and an excellent example. I'd urge you to get one – secondhand, for free on recycle websites (how we got one for our granddaughter) or by asking family and friends to club together.

Before we look at what you might feed your child it really helps to think about your own eating, and attitude to eating. They do what you do, not what you say. If you reward or bribe yourself with food – chocolate, cakes, a drink – even if you resolve not to give food as a reward or bribe to your children, they'll see you doing it to yourself, and get the idea. But the chances are, because there's so much pressure and expectation in our society to do so, that you may fall back on the idea that a sweet or ice cream, a cake or biscuit, is the best way to calm a fractious child and reward a good child. You'll notice when I talk about rewards it's always in the form of a non-edible treat.

If you swing between eating chips, crisps, fried food and sweet things and trying to eat healthy food, so will they. It's not rocket science; if you eat more calories than you use, you – and your children – will get fat. If you eat food that is pre-prepared, fried, full of fats and sugar, it will be really hard to stay below the calories in-calories out equation.

So if you want to help your kids, the options are clear:

▶ Get into the habit of using non-edible treats as rewards or bribes. For yourself it may be half an hour of having a quiet read, a bath, or listening to favourite music. For your child it may be an extra bedtime story, a chosen game, or a play in the park.
▶ Opt for healthy food. It may take time to get used to carrot sticks or a piece of fruit instead of biscuits, or low fat yoghurt instead of a cream pudding as dessert, but once you do you'll enjoy them.
▶ Don't make a big deal about it. Children pick up on anxiety. If you're stressed around the subject of food, the eating and sharing of food, you'll pass your uncertainties on to them.
▶ Don't take it personally. If children refuse certain foods or dishes, don't take it as a personal insult from them or failing on your part. It can be stingingly hurtful if they turn up their noses or express their displeasure, and several children together will urge each other on.

Children may seem to begin as blank slates when it comes to food. No child ever spits out breast milk saying 'Yuck!' They drink it with relish, mainly because it is designed to do the job, and because along with the nourishment comes love and security. When they move on to the food on spoons and in dishes, the trouble can begin. Some of this is because being fed, and learning to feed yourself, coincides with an awareness of self and those around you. Even small children in learning about what is around them want to manipulate and control it. Children want to play with their food, to examine and explore it. They want to be able to say yes, and no, to what we offer. They want to be in control. And they want to be able to express preferences, because with a wider choice of food comes the novel experience of taste.

Saying no

Food fads may well be part of a natural phase in a child's development – the chance to say no. They may try it out over food. Or over being strapped into a car or buggy seat. Or going to bed. Some try it out over just about everything – a few days ago I overheard a little girl happily burbling 'NO, no, NO, no, NONONO...' to herself, sitting in a supermarket trolley. Her very well clued in mother and I exchanged a rueful grin – she knew it was simply practice.

All toddlers go through a NO phase. Some take it way on into childhood, finally grow out of it only to reprise it, in adolescence. The fact that it occurs and however long it lasts it is a developmental stage, not an attack on you or the sign your child is being difficult. It IS difficult to manage, but they're not doing deliberately – and it will pass. There are some things you can do to cope, and to help make the phase as short as possible.

Tips to avoid NO battles

- ▶ Avoid saying NO yourself, as much as possible. Often, they get the idea from you and take it that much further on. Every no you say can set them off on a flurry of NOs themselves. Instead:
- ▶ Rather than saying 'No, you can't do that' offer a toy, point out something interesting, divert attention onto something else.
- ▶ Don't court NO by asking a yes or no question – always use open questions and offer choice. So, rather than 'Would you like a sandwich' ask 'Ham or cheese on your sandwich?'
- ▶ Promise for later. Instead of 'No, we can't do that' say 'After lunch/tonight/tomorrow/when dad gets home...' and make sure you do, so your child learns to trust you and such a promise.
- ▶ Offer alternatives. Instead of 'No! Don't write on the wall!' say 'Here's some paper, write on this instead!'
- ▶ Praise when they do something you like and ignore when they do something you don't. Remove them from whatever it is they're doing, but don't make a big deal about it, and find a good reason as soon as possible to praise them. If you maintain a positive attitude you can look for and see good behaviour.

Insight

Possibly the most important thing to remember – and make it your mantra through parenthood – is that It's Not Personal. When your child defies you, refuses the lovingly made meal, even says 'I hate you!' ... It's Not Personal. It's not about any shortcoming, failure or mistake on your part. It's Not Personal. It's about them, not you. It's about their struggle for independence, for self-expression, for competence and control. It's about their development, not your parenting. Repeat to yourself: It's Not Personal.

Acting up is about acting out

Children are happy when they feel good about themselves. One way of making a child feel good about themselves, of course, is to tell them how wonderful they are and how much you love them. But sometimes children are highly unlovable – they scream and refuse to do as they're told; they run around when you've asked them not to, and break things. They can be loving and sweet and charming. And then they can be angry and miserable, whiney and grumpy. And of course, they can have tantrums. Tantrums can happen at home, when a child throws themselves on the floor and kicks and screams or, in every parent's nightmare, in public. In the supermarket or a shop or car park or mall, with an audience. A staring, tut-tutting judgemental audience who all seem to be saying they know what your child needs and what are you going to do about it?

WHY DO THEY DO IT?

If you want to head off, stop or handle tantrums the first thing is to understand why they happen. A child in meltdown is likely to be:

A *frustrated child*. They know that shoelaces can be tied, that their favourite t-shirt is somewhere in the house but they can't find it, that certain words can be strung together to make you understand what they want. They can't quite do it – so they become overwhelmed and it comes out as anger at you, at themselves, at the world.

A *hungry or tired child*. Small children can't recognize either of these – wouldn't it be lovely if they could say 'I say Mama, I'm feeling a bit peckish and sleepy – how about a snack and a nap?' Instead, they say 'Waaaah!'

A *child wanting attention*. Kids want, need, love to be the centre of your attention, and if they can't be it by being quiet and good and well behaved, they'll command your notice by kicking off. You'd think no-one would want to be told off, but it's better than being ignored – or so a child feels.

A child told no. It may be that they want something – a sweet, a treat, some time with you. Or that you've asked them to play with someone else or to share a toy. 'No' can be their response to your 'No'.

An overloaded child. Picture your child as a cup. Normally, this cup is half full with emotions – the water – and half full with air – rational thoughts. When it's half and half you can reason with them. You can say 'We need to go shopping. Stay by me, hold my list and when we've finished if you've been quiet and done as I've asked we'll play.' And they can think about it and say yes. But sometimes the emotions start to fill up, pushing out the air and filling the cup with pure feelings. In such a state, they're overwhelmed and simply unable to think or respond rationally.

A child who wants to show they can manage. They're beginning to handle the world on their own terms and want to do certain things on their own. Picking them up, directing them to go where you want, strapping them into a car seat or buggy may be seen as deliberate thwarting of this natural aim, and they erupt.

SO HOW CAN YOU REDUCE TANTRUMS?

If you understand why a child is likely to go into meltdown, you can take measures to head them off at the pass. These can include:

- ▶ Positive parenting. The more you praise your child and notice when they do the right thing while ignoring when they do things you don't want, the more likely they are to lean towards behaviour they know you like.
- ▶ Give them some control. Since many tantrums are about feeling out of control, help your child by giving them some choices in their life. That doesn't mean handing over power to children – that's not helpful, it's scary. But being able to pick between two items – the red socks or blue, fish or pasta for lunch – can make an enormous difference.
- ▶ Managing trouble spots. You'll learn by experience the times and places where and when your child finds it hard to cope – the first ten minutes after coming home, or in supermarkets. Concentrate on finding ways of managing those times and places.

▶ Model what you want. Sounds obvious but it's amazing how often we forget that children copy us. They do what we do, not what we say! If when you get stressed you explode, then so will your child. You may need to work on managing your own temper and ways of handling pressure.

▶ Learn the signs. Most children give you full warning they're building up, being whiney, crotchety, sulky. That is the time to stop, think what's going on and try either distraction, engagement or negotiation.

DEAL WITH THEM!

What if in spite of all your efforts – or because you were distracted and missed the signs – your child kicks off? How should you react to the full scale volcano that is a red faced, screaming, crying, kicking child in a tantrum?

Be sympathetic. Yes, I know that's hard because you need sympathy yourself having to deal with this. But the child is in the grip of powerful feelings they cannot understand or control. See them as a victim of something they cannot control and you can feel their pain, and be better adjusted to help them.

Keep calm. Hard, I know, but taking a deep breath and calming your own racing heart and shattered nerves will help both of you. You'll be better able to cope, and will show your child you're balanced, which is what they need when they feel out of control.

Try to turn it off. If you can be quick enough and the tantrum is only just beginning, using distraction or ignoring it might nip it in the bud. Walk away, look out of the window, offer a toy or snack. But don't feel you've failed if it's already in flow and you can't stop it.

Snuggle. Since your child is feeling overwhelmed and probably terrified of the power of their feelings, being held calmly and firmly often helps. Get on the ground with the child, envelope them in a bear hug and talk calmly and soothingly. Note however, with some children or at some times this can be felt as controlling or belittling and they may fight against it.

Time out. If your child is over 18 months old, you can use a time out. Remove them from the situation – put them into a quiet room or strapped into their seat in the car – and walk away so you can recover and so can they. Stay away for no more than two minutes: time enough for them to know they've been left to calm down but not long enough to feel abandoned – time it!

Set it aside. Once the tantrum has passed over like a wet and windy squall, forget it. Cuddle, make up and move on.

Potty training

Once you've seen how routines can help, as can letting children take the lead and show you what they want, you will want to use those strategies on the step that some parents and children find so difficult – potty training. The very phrase is a mistake because in the best scenario, you're not training – the child is working it out for themselves when they're ready, with your support.

Having your child dry at night and able to use, and signal when they want to use, a potty, then the toilet, is one of those things that can prove more elusive the more you focus on it. Learning how tends to begin to happen around the age of two. It tends not to be able to happen before the age of 20 months because before then, children don't have the control of their bladders that this requires. If you push it – especially if you respond to someone telling you they managed it when their child was crawling, or are in a hurry to get them dry before a new baby or some other family change – you're likely to make the situation fraught and the process lengthy. Your toddler is the person whose lead you should follow – they'll tell you when they're ready.

Your child may be ready when they:

▶ show interest when family members use the toilet
▶ let you know their nappy is dirty and they want to be changed
▶ tend to stay dry for a couple of hours each day
▶ make it obvious they're having a bowel movement in their nappy
▶ have bowel movements at regular times of the day, such as after breakfast or when getting ready for bed.

Top tips
▶ See it, and approach it with your child, as an adventure and an advantage. This is an exciting move forward, not a struggle.
▶ Take your time. The later you leave it, and the more you let it be something your child has chosen to do, the quicker it is likely to happen.

- Expect a step back for every two steps forward. It's just a skill like every other – you expected them to fall over often when learning to walk.
- Prepare for the learning experience by making sure clothes are easy to pull down and using training pants.
- Take your child to choose their potty, and toilet seat. The more they see it as an exciting development and a new toy and game to play, the more they want to take part.
- Be ready for your child, having received the new potty with great excitement, to ignore it. Don't force, bribe, cajole or try to humiliate a child into using it – that will only set up either fear or defiance. Have it around and when they are ready, they'll use it.
- Give lots of praise when they do use it.
- Don't show disappointment or anger if there's an accident. Change the child, clear up any mess and say cheerfully 'Never mind! You'll get there...'
- They may want to examine, boast about and show you the contents of the potty and expect you to be impressed and pleased. Be impressed and pleased. And they may find flushing the toilet when they have finished either scary or distressing. Leave it until they've gone back to playing elsewhere.
- Dry in the day, and being able to hold back until on the loo or potty, is much easier than making it through the night. Be prepared for training pants at night, and for you to have to 'lift' the child before you go to bed, for some time after they have mastered daytime.

Exercise

Think about the last time you and your toddler clashed. Get paper and pencils and write down:

A (Adult)

C (Child)

T (Tools)

Fill in – what was going on for you, what do you think might be going on for your child and lastly what might have been the tools you could use?

To give you an even better idea of what is happening, draw a Behaviour, Feelings, Needs Fountain for yourself, and for your child. When things get rough, ask:

▶ What is the behaviour? What do you, and your child, do? Shout, sulk, have a tantrum, stamp away? What does your child do?
▶ What are the feelings? Underneath the behaviour, what might be the emotions? Anger, jealousy, grief, guilt?
▶ What could be the needs? Even deeper down, is there a wish to be loved and noticed, fear of rejection, a wish to be valued?

KEY POINTS

1 The toddler years are the best time to lay down the foundations of your parenting skills that will see you through the rest of your child's development until they eventually leave you as well-prepared young adults.

2 Understanding what it is like to be a toddler – putting yourself in their shoes – will help you through this demanding time.

3 ACT (Adult, Child, Tools), not react, can be a major help here and stop any situation spinning out of control.

4 Trying to understand what is behind a toddler's behaviour, sharing their play and 'respecting the struggle' are further invaluable aids towards having enjoyable and successful toddler years.

5 The transition from baby to toddler is understandably challenging. But it can also allow a chance to 'ease off' a bit – and perhaps get a little bit of your life back for you and your partner.

6 You can be an authoritarian parent, a permissive one or a positive one. The first two have definite downsides so a self-aware, positive approach would seem to be the best way to go.

7 Try to be realistic about your expectations over such issues as routines, bedtimes and reading, But once you've made a rule, don't give in.

8 There are paths through the minefield of the dreadful 'NO' – whether it is you or your child saying it. Try looking again at the alternatives given in this chapter and also consider that not entering into any arguments in the first place can be a very effective way of defusing potential clashes.

9 The toddler years could just as easily be called the tantrum years. Again, it will help to go back and re-read the tips for dealing with them – they may well save your sanity!

10 It might seem impossible to do at times, but keep your sense of humour. However, never laugh *at* a child as it would be hurtful and only make matters worse.

BEING HAPPY

How are you doing with the fun sheet? Here are a few more ideas to add – do your own!

Small things	Medium things	Big things
Start a blog. Share a cup of coffee with your partner. Watch your toddler play. Make hot buttered crumpets.	Go window shopping with a friend. Make a new friend. Take your toddler swimming. Sit with your partner over a bottle of wine when the kids are in bed and sort out the world.	Meet up with old friends for a night out. Go for a day by the seaside. Make a train trip with plenty of toys and drawing materials for your child. Get a pet.

4

The child

In this chapter you will learn:
- *Listening and other skills*
- *How to set family rules and have family round table discussions*
- *About positive parenting*
- *How important you are to your children*

This is the period when increased communication between parent and child becomes possible as they become able to make themselves fully understood, and when communication between you and them and the whole family becomes so important. Shared family time gives you the opportunity to keep your lines of communication open, to listen to ideas, to welcome joys and triumphs, to allow worries and concerns to be raised in a safe space and to pass on important messages. All this happens so much more easily, and so much more enjoyably, if your family have a routine of being together – round a table for a meal, sharing games, playing and reading together. Sadly, we know that many children in developed countries such as the UK and US say that their parents often only talk to them to tell them off or interrogate them, and that shared family times seem to have declined. It's no surprise then to discover that children in the UK and US are found to be much unhappier than children in countries such as Norway and the Netherlands, where children say they and their parents often 'just chat' together.

It's good to talk

Children need at this time to bring issues about school and friends, about what they are learning about themselves and those around them, to their parents. For babies and toddlers, parents are the main focus of their lives. But as soon as children start to mix with others in toddler groups they begin to widen their horizons. When they go to primary school, friends begin to assume a significance and children need to show their parents that they have personalities and tastes of their own, and that the opinions of friends assumes an increasing importance to them, and to have this accepted. This not only has significance in the development of children, it impinges on parents and their confidence and self-esteem, their relationship with their children and view of where they stand with them. In effect, it is the beginning of separation.

CHOSEN ADULTS

Children may also begin to have 'chosen adults' – teachers or other professionals they come into contact with, other relatives, neighbours, the parents of friends – to whom they go and who they look up to, and may quote or refer to. However, as children in effect begin to move away from parents, they need to know they have a safety net and that their parents' marriage/relationship is safe and secure. The demands of being a parent to a toddler or a young child may be the very thing that begins to drive a wedge between a couple, to create a situation where your children's needs become paramount. Your children are important and often you can't put their needs aside. But equally, if you sideline your own relationship until they are older, you may come back to find it's died in the meantime. Focus on your children by all means. But don't lose sight of each other and your need to keep in touch as a couple.

LISTENING AND TALKING

Insight
My favourite parental observation was made by a comedian who watched a woman in a crowded tube train with a child who was saying 'Mum! Mum! Mum! Mum! Mum! Mum! Mum! Mum! Mum!' seemingly on an endless loop. After a few minutes, apparently the mother looked heavenwards and sighed 'I can't believe how happy I was the first time you said that...'

You'll be so happy when your children start to talk. You'll be so frustrated as they struggle with their own frustration in trying to make themselves understood. And soon enough you'll be driven to distraction either trying to shut them up when it gets too much, or open them up when they won't talk. As they begin their first words, now is the time to set in place skills and techniques to listen effectively, communicate successfully and talk to them meaningfully.

THE ART OF LISTENING

There is an art to listening. Three techniques which you may have heard about are often suggested as useful with adults, or teenagers. In fact, the sooner you begin using them the better. They help you, in getting into practice with effective and helpful listening. And they help your child not only by encouraging the skills of expressing themselves but by helping them feel you will hear them and that they have something worth saying.

The three main techniques are Active Listening, Reflective Listening and Open Questions.

Active Listening

In the first two techniques the key is keeping quiet ourselves while encouraging the other person to feel able to talk to us. With Active Listening, we use body language to make it clear our focus and attention is on the other person. We use eye contact, turn towards them, crouch down if necessary to be on the same level. We give full attention, not half an eye and ear while doing something else. We avoid crossing our arms (which gives the impression that we're closed off from them). Then, as the person speaks we don't interrupt but make the sort of noises – ums and ahs and uh-huhs – and nods that indicate we are listening and want them to go on.

Reflective Listening

With Reflective Listening we go one step further. The body language is the same and the no interruption rules remain. But now we check out that we've understood by repeating back what they've said to us 'So you're saying...am I right in thinking you mean...' With young children struggling to use words or string sentences together, we'd simply say their words back to them. And we don't laugh or make fun of their attempts and are patient as they make their efforts.

Discover the power of using Active and Reflective Listening with your partner. Toss a coin for who goes first. The one going first gets two minutes having the floor, being able to talk without interruptions. The task for the other is to use active listening to encourage them on – making eye contact, nodding and umm-ing and ah-ing to let them know they are paying full attention. Then, swap over. Then, try it again with Reflective Listening, the listener repeating back and checking out. When you've each had a go talk it over – how did it feel to be given a free rein knowing you weren't going to be interrupted? How did it feel to use both active and reflective skills? How did it feel to have active and reflective skills used by the other person?

Open questions

Open questions are important mainly because they are the opposite of what can kill a conversation, a Closed Question. A Closed Question is one which can be answered by yes, no or just a grunt. In fact, not only does it not encourage more, it positively begs to be snapped off short with a one word retort plus a full stop. Instead with an Open Question we make sure we encourage children to think about what they might say and answer as fully as possible.

A Closed Question might be 'Did you have fun in school today?' An Open Question would be 'Tell me about your day!' Closed Questions also tend to steer children down the avenue of enquiry we've chosen. When you leave it open you might be surprised what they choose to tell you, ask you, and share with you.

HOW DO WE MANAGE WHEN CHILDREN FIND IT HARD?

There are several common issues with children trying to make themselves understood or heard.

Children may know what they want but can't find the words. But often, we can tell if we pay attention. Bad behaviour is always about bad feelings so a child acting up, whining or crying, usually has a need that cries out to be fulfilled. Use your knowledge of them and coax them by offering words yourself to find the problem. Think ACT, and the Behaviour, Feelings, Needs Fountain (see Chapter 3).

▶ Children often interrupt what you're doing or when you're talking to someone else, especially if you're on the phone. If it happens again and again you may need to ask yourself if all these other involvements are as necessary as your child, and whether you need to focus more on them. After all, what's more important? If however you feel the child is being demanding, say 'Wait. It's adult time/I have to finish this. I'll be with you in a moment.' When you can find a good moment for them, say 'Now – what was that?'

▶ Children often feel they can't wait – to them, it's now or never. And they might fear they'll forget what it was they wanted to say or how to say it if they can't get it out RIGHT NOW. You may need to pay attention if they're struggling. If you think they've got to the point where it's a valuable lesson, say 'Hold that thought until I'm ready.' If it's gone, next time teach them to repeat it to themselves until you can give them attention.

▶ Children can get into the habit of whining or whinging. It often works – it's like a nail on a shiny surface and we respond to stop it. That, of course, in the long run only results in their using it again since it works. Instead, say 'Nice voice, please. I can't make out what you're saying if you do it in that voice.'

Insight

It's worth becoming aware of your own tone when speaking to your children. If you often sound impatient, annoyed or sarcastic, your children will be less inclined to listen to you. A friend's small daughter once, in my presence, said rather tartly to her annoyed mother 'Nice voice, Mummy, please…' We had to agree she had a point – I know my friend took more care with her tone after that. After all, they do what you do, not what you say – if you want certain behaviour you have to model it.

▶ Children may seem to talk non-stop. Endless questions, endless prattle. It's easy sometimes to want to tune out to get some peace. But this phase doesn't last as long as you think. Once they get to be teenagers, or even as tweens, they might not talk – or at least, not to you. Make the most of it, with patience and a smile. It's good to be the centre of someone's world.

▶ Children sometimes don't want to talk. Once they move out into the world and make friends of their own they may want to keep them to themselves. Or they may feel conflicted at the division between playgroup, nursery or school and home, and be attempting to keep them apart, to keep them straight in their own mind. You may need to use open questions, and active and reflective listening to help them feel safe and open up.

Self-esteem

What do we mean by self-esteem? It's when a child feels good about themselves. Not 'I'm better than you' and certainly not 'I'm not as good as you' or even 'I'm only OK if somebody tells me so.' Self-esteem is 'I'm OK because I know I am'. We help our children grow their self-esteem by giving praise, by encouraging them to do their best and to recognize their own abilities and positive characteristics. Above all, we help them to be able to see their own worth without needing other people to validate it. A child with good self-esteem is a confident child, a generous and sympathetic child and, above all, a happy child.

OVERPRAISING OUR CHILDREN

But there is a balance, and overpraising children can be as counterproductive as not praising them. We seem to have initiated, quite properly, a backlash against the old style belief that praising children spoiled them and made them soft or complacent. But we seem to have replaced that with parents who praise their child for doing the least little thing. Praise can raise a child's confidence and make them feel good about themselves – obviously, A Good Thing – and can also give them the incentive to earn your notice and your approval again. But overpraising can have the opposite effect. Praise a child for simply being, and not only do they can get the idea that you expect the best results every time, but they doubt their own ability to do so. After all, if they couldn't quite see what it was they did to earn that praise, how can they repeat it?

DESCRIPTIVE PRAISE

But what is praise? We often think saying 'Well done, you!' is what is needed. And that's all very nice, but it doesn't work if it's given with a sour look, or if we follow it up with '...but why didn't you do it before I asked you to?' And it's no good if the child actually knows you don't mean it, or they don't really deserve it. So, praise is when we make a positive comment, in a warm and kind tone of voice, with a loving look, and it's genuine. And the best praise is Descriptive Praise.

Descriptive Praise is when you say clearly what it was they did that pleased you. The more precise your description, the better they know what you liked and know you are pleased. The child now knows they can do this task and can repeat it another time and earn more praise. It feels a bit odd to do this, and can take some practice. But when you see how effective it is you'll realize it's worth doing.

Instead of 'Well done! What a good boy' you say 'You cleared up all your toys and put them away in the right boxes. The living room looks really tidy. Thank you!'

Here are some good phrases to use, to praise:

▶ Thank you for that. You did this...and then you did that... That was really helpful/kind/useful.
▶ I love playing with you. You're a good sport because you keep the rules and don't try to cheat.
▶ You used your imagination when you drew that picture.
▶ You worked really hard to do that – well done!
▶ You kept on and didn't give up.
▶ You showed kindness – thank you!
▶ Are you pleased with yourself? You should be!
▶ Are you proud of what you did? You should be!
▶ I like it when you...
▶ I like the way you...
▶ I thought it was really good when you...
▶ I could see you were trying hard
▶ Look at how you...
▶ I can trust you to...because you...

Insight

Children should learn how to fail. In fact, they need to get the message from us that they should feel good about being wrong. That's because failing is the best way of learning a lesson. If you get it wrong and messed up this time, that's the way to learn how to do it differently next time. You don't succeed by always succeeding because sooner or later you are going to come up against something you can't do first time, and how do you know how to be resilient and try again, if you haven't had to do it?

Using your skills to have happy times together

So far we have looked at communication skills and setting limits, and often we can see how to apply these in specific, almost crisis moments – the tantrums around a shopping trip, the arguments around bedtime. What can be difficult is seeing our way through managing the day to day, drip-drip-drip events that might not feel like a big conflict but add up to stress and conflict. It's easier if a parent is at home full time, or before children begin nursery or school. But once at least one of you works and your child spends part or all of the day away from you that half hour when you get back together as a family in the evening can be fraught. Getting food on the table can seem a priority, as everyone and children especially will be hungry. And it always seems as if there is an argument or meltdown just waiting to happen. So how do you start family time in a happy mood, and keep it happy?

SEE THE PROBLEM

You've just had a busy day and may still have issues, responsibilities and tasks from that on your mind. It can be vital for you to put your work and day-self aside in order for you to be available to your children as a parent. One good tactic is to change clothes between day gear and evening, helping you change personas from daytime mode to evening. Even changing from one set of jeans to another, or jeans to joggers, makes that division. Business suit to casual gear really sets the tone. Another, if you have the time, is to have a shower, both symbolically and literally washing away the day. A third is to set aside just five minutes between your day duties and taking on the children to sit still and listen to music, on your way, or at, home. Have a cup of coffee, breathe deeply, relax. If one of you is at home during the day they can look after the kids while you de-stress and get ready and then you can take over while they have their few minutes off too. If both of you are arriving home from work, give each other the opportunity to do this.

FILL YOUR CUP

This is an important technique to help you be able, happy and willing to give as much of yourself as possible to your children. Think of yourself as a cup. If your cup is full when your partner and your children come running to you and ask for a sip, or a gulp and a swallow, you can say 'Of course! I'm full to the brim – help yourself!' If your cup is half full you have to say 'Well, I'd love you to have a drink but be careful – there's only so much there.' And if your cup is empty, you have to say 'No! Go away! I've got nothing – none for me, none for you!' If you've left yourself feeling tired, fed up, resentful and drained, your cup is empty. You can't give time, love and attention to your family because you're too drained to do so properly. You need to fill your cup by taking care of yourself. In that five minutes before joining your family take a moment to think of all the things you did in the day you can feel pleased and proud about. Think about the fun you can now have with your children. And plan the quiet time after they have gone to bed when you can have some adult time – promise yourself just one good treat that will relax and reward you, such as a bath, a favourite TV programme, time to talk and catch up, or some romance. Make a decision at this point to do something for yourself tomorrow and later in the week that will refresh and renew you.

When you see your family, three things will transform the situation, heading off conflict and helping you all reconnect:

▶ Love them
▶ Feed them
▶ Listen to them

Love them
Your kids, and your partner, will be looking forward to seeing you after the day, but you can set the reconnection into a positive, or a negative mode simply with your first contact. If it's to launch into reminding them of things they have to do, or with complaints, or simply by giving them half, or none, of your attention as you dash around, they can be forgiven for feeling let down. Whether they came home in a good mood or a bad one, the result is likely to be at best neutral, at worst heading for a row. But even if when they first saw you they, or you, were feeling down, if your reaction is to make eye contact and greet them lovingly with a hug and kiss, the result is likely to be positive. However you actually feel, make the effort to begin the evening on a high note and it will stay that way.

Feed them
Kids and adults feel hungry after a busy day. If all focus is on a meal that needs preparing, by the time it's ready it may be too late. For a start, making that meal takes up your time and attention – time

and attention that should be spent on your family. So the best thing to do is to begin with a snack that can be rustled up immediately – crackers and cheese, a dip and a plate of carrot and other vegetable sticks you cut up in the morning and left ready, fruit slices, or a smoothie. You could offer biscuits or cake but that may be a dose of sugar too far, while the other ideas can be seen as the first course of your evening meal.

Listen to them

Everyone may be bursting with things they want to tell you and share, or worries they need to discuss. Ask open-ended questions to set the tone – all of you share what you did today that you enjoyed, found hard, found easy, want to repeat, want to do better. Eye to eye, focused attention around the table can gradually give way to listening as you do other things, but you need to start it off by being there with them, and for them.

KEEP FOCUSED

One important message to give your family is that they come first and they matter. And one way you might diffuse this message is if you turn away to communicate with other people, or let them do the same. So for this golden half hour of getting back together, ban connection outside. Turn your mobile off, or silence it and park it by the front door as you come in, and ask anyone else who has one in your family to do the same. Don't check emails or social media for messages; don't go online. If they've brought anything back from nursery or school for your attention, put it aside for later. After you've eaten may be the time for your children to watch a programme or film or play games and for you to check for important messages – once they've gone to bed is the time to get back to purely social enquiries – but for now, be a family, together, with no outside distractions.

KEEP THEM WITH YOU

After the first 'getting back together' time, and when everyone has had the edge of hunger taken off, get on with preparing the evening meal. But try to keep your kids with you. Often, we want some peace and quiet ourselves or feel they might get in the way, so we send them off to their own rooms or into the living room, to watch TV or play. It seems like a good idea. But how often does it actually lead to further problems? We may need to be constantly popping out to supervise in case they're getting up to mischief. Or when we want them to come back, we have battles to turn off whatever has seized their attention. A better idea might be to set up a routine where they stay with you. If still young, they can draw and colour at the kitchen table as you cook. If they have homework, they can do it then and there – a good habit to instil. Or, they can help. This has several advantages. Cooking together is a highly bonding experience. You can play guessing games to name ingredients and talk about where they come from. It also encourages healthy eating. If you know you're going to have your children watch, take part and learn how, you might be encouraged to make meals from scratch – stir fries, stews, various mince dishes, pasta and different sauces. All give you the opportunity to let your children enjoy taking ingredients out of cupboards and the fridge, to cut them up, mix them in and see what makes real food. You're far less likely to get 'Yuck! This is icky! Don't want to eat it!' from a child who has helped you make a spaghetti sauce than one who just has it plunked in front of them.

WHAT IF ONE PARTNER GETS HOME LATE?

Feed children at the time that is best for them. That might mean you eating earlier than you prefer. And it may mean one of you misses out on sitting down for a main meal in the evening. There are two opposing needs here, so let's look at how to prioritize. It's really, really important for family cohesion and happiness that you have as many meals as possible together, seated round a table. But it's equally vital that small children get fed early, and get to bed on time. So you can do one of several things:

▶ While they are young, arrange work responsibilities so you can all be home early. That might seem extreme, but what is more important? Setting the foundations of a strong, connected family now may not just avoid heartache and problems later, it may be cost-effective too. Unhappy, warring families are actually potentially very expensive!

▶ Separate your mealtimes. Whoever is at home eats with the kids; whoever comes later eats on their own.

▶ Separate your meals. Whoever is at home snacks while the kids eat their main course and eats with whoever comes home later. Or, whoever is at home eats a main course with the kids but saves dessert to share with whoever comes home later. Even better, all at home save dessert to share with whoever comes home later.

The key point is this: eating together round a table is good for families and good for children. Do whatever it takes to set this as a habit for later life, when you can all sit down in the evening to share a meal. The earlier you start making this a 'given' and instilling such habits the better.

IF MUSIC BE THE FOOD OF LOVE...

Putting on soothing music can also help set the tone, and calm everyone down. Avoid anything too energetic. Your children may want something they can dance to but avoid that – it will only get them up and keep the daytime vibe going. You want them to slow down, so choose something dreamy and quiet.

Family rules

Every family should come up with a set of House or Family Rules. There are several reasons for this. One is that, whether you realize it or not, every family has some rules they live by. Sometimes, these have been discussed and everyone knows them. Sometimes, they're sort-of known and sort-of agreed. Often, they do exist but people aren't always sure what they are exactly. Of course, rules do change from time to time, as children grow or as you realize there are new circumstances that warrant them. Sitting down together and discussing Family or House Rules means you have to discuss them, agree them and learn what they are. Then there's no excuse for anyone not realizing what they should or should not be doing.

By talking the Rules through and allowing even young children to have their say, you get two results. One is that everyone should 'buy in to' the rules. You set them, you had a chance to make them or alter them, now you keep them. And this means all members of the house get a say – even young children too. For every rule that the adults want on there, there should be one the children put forward.

Rules and boundaries are things that parents have to set and supervise so they are kept. It's one of the tasks of adulthood and parenthood and if our family, our children and we ourselves are going to be happy we need to accept this charge. But as children get older you can begin to ask for consensus. That doesn't mean the buck stops with anyone but you – you're still in ultimate responsibility. But it does mean that by discussing rules with your children you can be more effective. How does this work?

FAMILY ROUND TABLE

Having Family Round Table meetings are something all families benefit from, and while it may seem difficult to put into action when children are young you'd be surprised at what a young age they can respond well to such a strategy. It's a skill all parents need to foster in themselves and their children, so the earlier you try it, practise it and get used to it the better. Family Round Tables mean all sitting down together and agreeing to listen and not interrupt and to let everyone have their say and to be listened to with respect. It often helps to have an object you can pass round that signals who 'has the floor' and is speaking.

You might like to make the first order of business a set of agreed rules for how you run Family Round Tables. Here's a list of rules three young children came up with for their family:

- ▶ No answering back
- ▶ No pushing each other, or pinching
- ▶ Be kind to each other
- ▶ Always come to the meeting on time and be smiley
- ▶ No being rude or burping
- ▶ Be sensible
- ▶ No storming off
- ▶ Let others talk and don't interrupt
- ▶ Put your hand up when you want to speak
- ▶ Keep your temper
- ▶ Don't bring arguments into the meeting – settle them before
- ▶ No shouting or swearing

There's a lot of 'Nos' there that I might like to turn into positives... but it gets the point across!

RECOGNIZING THE REASONS FOR RULES

Another result of talking through the Rules is that setting them helps young people as well as adults think about why they are needed and what might be the effect of having – or not having – them.

Sometimes, it helps adults realize priorities. With young children you may want to keep all the rules you set, such as making their bed at the beginning of the day, and tidying up toys at the end, because instilling routines and good habits is important. As they get older however you may decide to let go a little on their personal territory. Tidying up in the living room stands because it affects everyone but whether they make their own bed can be their own choice. The point being that as children grow up if you kick up a major fuss over the less important things, you lose out on being able to say 'No, this one really IS important' for the vital issues. Discussing rules allows you to choose your battles. And you'll be surprised how sensible even very young people can be, given the responsibility and the option.

SETTING FAMILY RULES

You set House or Family Rules by all getting together round a table with a big sheet of paper and some pens. This is the preliminary stage – you're not looking for perfection or neatness at this point. Appoint someone to be the note taker – give this task to a child if they can manage it. And then Ideas Storm.

Ideas Storming
Ideas Storming is putting down EVERYTHING that comes to mind. Ask 'What House or Family Rules do we think we already have? What House or Family Rules do we want?' You might also ask 'What problems do we have and how could we do something about them?'

Write down every single suggestion. Even if you think them unworkable, silly, or too difficult to manage. The only thing you should exclude might be rules that anyone suggests with the intention of 'getting at' another member of the family. So, 'No coming in and messing up my toys' when said by one child and directed at another isn't acceptable. But 'Everyone to ask before using anyone else's belongings' is fair – it applies to all.

Consider your ideas
Having written everything down, the second stage is: look at and consider them. Think about what you all want to achieve. Some of your rules may be about getting on with each other – about being nice and helpful. You might put in a rule about not swearing, hitting, fighting, or shouting. Some may be about running the home smoothly – you might have a family rule about always taking

shoes off at the door, or always hanging coats up when you come in or always washing up your own cups or putting them in the dishwasher. Some may be about big and important things such as crossing roads safely or never unbuckling seat belts in the car. As your children get older you might add rules about teenagers always carrying mobiles when they're out at night with friends and never getting into a car with a driver who's been drinking.

Choosing rules
The third stage is agreeing which rules you will choose to be your House or Family Rules. You might like to rewrite rules to make them as constructive as possible – that is, use 'Dos' rather than 'Don'ts'. Be as specific as possible – a vague rule about respecting people is less helpful that saying people should listen to each other, not shout them down, interrupt or call them names. You may find you have some overlapping rules – prune or combine. You may have some you don't like, and some the children don't like. Make your case and listen to theirs. And do some 'Horse Trading' – this rule stays in if I say yes to that one.

Then, write them out neatly. Agree you will all keep them – you might like to draw up a contract that says so, and ALL (adults included) sign it. Hang up the House or Family Rules and the contract somewhere you can all see them.

Revisit them regularly – maybe once a week. Are they working? If not, why not? What needs to be changed so they will work?

Some suggested rules
Here are some suggested rules you might consider:

▶ Shoes off at the door and always hang coats up
▶ Leave lunch box in kitchen to be washed
▶ If you want a snack, ask and then clear up after yourselves or ask for help
▶ Do your chores with no arguments
▶ Talk with each other instead of shouting at each other
▶ No kicking, hitting, shoving, biting, swearing or shouting
▶ Share toys and games but the owner has right to go first
▶ Be kind, be positive, praise often and always say Please, Thank You and Well Done
▶ If you want someone to hear you, you have to listen to them

- ▶ Help people do better instead of being nasty to them
- ▶ Dad to come home early on Friday
- ▶ Watch a new film together every Sunday
- ▶ Go to bed at agreed times
- ▶ Pocket money to be given every Friday night
- ▶ Special chores can earn more pocket money

Chores

So, what about chores? The first chore a child will do is tidy up their own toys. It's an important task for several reasons. It helps them because it signals the end of a day's play – part of the bedtime routine that draws a line under playtime and daytime and ushers in night-time by clearing games away. But it also helps because it tells them that there are some tasks they should do for themselves, rather than expect you to do for them. And it makes them an active member of the family rather than a passive one and gives them some control in their environment. Parents sometimes feel it's unfair to burden children with such work – they should live innocent, free, unencumbered lives. That misses several points:

- ▶ Young children often want to help – they see it as a game, and a way of being like you.
- ▶ It gives them some power over their surroundings. Tidying their room and making their own bed gives them the opportunity to set it up the way they like rather than the way you may choose.
- ▶ You aren't a slave or a servant, put on earth to look after everyone else. When children do chores from an early age, they have a respect for you and appreciate what it takes to keep a home running.
- ▶ When everyone pulls their weight it means everyone can have some free time. Having you do it all means that one person is tired and sometimes resentful. Shared responsibility means you have more time to have fun together.
- ▶ Sometime soon, children will leave to run their own homes. Leaving comes as more of a shock, and can end in disaster, if they haven't acquired the skills to look after themselves and a recognition of what it takes. The earlier they start making some contribution, the more they will accept it as a 'given'.

AT WHAT AGE CAN THEY DO WHICH CHORES?

Clearly, there are things that a ten-year-old can do that it would be entirely inappropriate to ask a four-year-old to attempt. But equally, having started children off at two or three, it's wrong to think it stops there – as they get older so too does their ability to manage more tasks. Children can:

- ▶ At two to three:
    - ▷ put toys away
    - ▷ put dirty clothes in the laundry basket
    - ▷ help feed a pet
    - ▷ pick out their own clothes.
- ▶ At four to five:
    - ▷ feed a pet
    - ▷ clean up spillages
    - ▷ get dressed
    - ▷ make their bed
    - ▷ clear the table after a meal
    - ▷ help empty the dishwasher.
- ▶ At six to seven:
    - ▷ sort laundry
    - ▷ sweep a floor
    - ▷ set the table
    - ▷ help make meals
    - ▷ clean their bedroom.
- ▶ At eight to nine:
    - ▷ load the dishwasher
    - ▷ put away groceries
    - ▷ put away laundry
    - ▷ walk the dog
    - ▷ prepare their breakfast (and yours too, on Mother's or Father's Day!).
- ▶ At ten to twelve:
    - ▷ wash the car
    - ▷ do the laundry
    - ▷ iron clothes.
- ▶ As teenagers:
    - ▷ make a meal
    - ▷ do the shopping
    - ▷ clean the bathroom and kitchen.

You'd supervise a two- to three-year-old, keep a watch over a four- to five-year-old, but by the time your children get to six and seven you would expect to be able to trust them to be responsible and do what's necessary on their own – if, that is, they have been given the steer by you from that early age that this is what we do in a family.

HOW TO BEGIN

How do we approach introducing chores if it hasn't been done from an early age?

▶ Firstly, stop thinking of it as something you're getting or asking them to do. What will happen is that all of you will have a discussion about what it takes to keep a home running, and the children are going to recognize that you have enough on your plate and can't do it all. They are going to see that if they live here and expect their clothes to be cleaned and food to be put on the table, some sharing out of chores needs to be done. It's not an argument or a request – it's a recognition of realities. When you simply put it that this will be done – full stop, no argument – kids usually fall in. Especially if they understand how much you need their help and how much it will mean that they can be relied upon.

▶ Secondly, start trusting them. It may take some time to work out and begin but the work is all in the setting up. After that, you gain so much time since you're not doing it all.

▶ Thirdly, you have to accept that some tasks will not be done to your exacting standards. It's vital you get your priorities right: does it matter that the dusting is done so the house gleams all day every day, or that you can sit down and share a coffee with your kids and chat because you don't have to do it all?

HOW TO DRAW UP A CHORE CHART

How should you draw up a chore chart? For it to be something that everyone 'buys into' and agrees, it's best to make it a co-operative effort. But it does help for one person in the family to take responsibility for managing it and making it run. That doesn't have to be one of the adults; you can delegate this to your teenager, as a way of further enlisting their co-operation and sense of ownership. To forestall arguments you could rotate this, asking each young person to take responsibility for a week or a month at a time. Have a family discussion and agree:

- ▶ What are the routine chores that need doing? These could be washing-up or feeding and walking family pets, filling the dishwasher, loading the washing machine, laying tables, vacuuming the living room, and so on.
- ▶ Decide which chores have to be done, come what may. Different families have different ideas of what's important – come to your own agreement.
- ▶ Decide which chores are quick and easy, and which are long and hard.
- ▶ Draw up a list of chores, and assign them. You might like to give everyone a mix of easy, medium and hard chores for each time period. Or you might opt for each person having easy, medium or hard weeks. You'll find some children like, and even fight for, some chores or hate others, and not all agree on which.
- ▶ You might also want to agree on what might be 'extra' chores, such as washing cars or mowing lawns, and negotiate whether these can be done as paid-for jobs. Some families may want to tie chores into pocket money – you get it if you complete your chores, or the amount you get is dependent on chores.

Agree what you're going to do, and then draw up a written agreement or contract setting it out. Ask everyone to sign the contract: 'We, the undersigned, agree…' Review the contract regularly and if it's not working, go back to the table to discuss why and what you'd like to do to make it work.

Routines

We've talked already about the importance of having certain specific routines – bedtime routines, routines to help fend off the supermarket tantrum. But it's worth reflecting on why routines are so important to you and your family. Children need structure. You'd think they'd love chaos and freedom, because that's what they seem to delight in or constantly push for. But the reality is that kids push boundaries because they want you to show them their limits. A limit can be seen as something that holds you in. In fact, it's something that holds the bad stuff out, and protects you, and children instinctively know that.

CHANGE CAN BE HARD

Structure is about managing change. We all have to live with change, and we all find it hard. Even a change to something better can be regarded as difficult, simply because it's unknown, and different from what we're used to. Moving to a new home, or starting a new job, may be eagerly anticipated and deliberately brought about, but will still cause stress. But for children this shock of the new occurs so much more often. Think about it. As a young child, there is so much to handle in such a short time. Their body is changing, altering in size and shape. They go from home to child minder, to playgroup to nursery to school in such a short time. They have to learn to walk, talk, read, and maybe to ride a bike, swim, climb trees and cross roads. Even day by day they have to cope with new foods, new sights and sounds, new demands and experiences. No wonder occasionally they want to stop dead and say 'NO!'

Seven reasons to keep to a routine with your children:

It puts kids in control

If you have a set routine of bedtimes, getting up times, mealtimes, and playtimes, your children know what is expected. Which means after a time they can be the ones to remind you and to run their own schedule. It's when you constantly get on their case to tell them to tidy their room, take off their shoes when indoors, get ready for a meal, that they get stroppy and defiant.

It gets rid of power struggles

If you have to constantly remind them, ask them, shout at them to do this and do that you're one step away from a fight. You're the nasty parent nagging at them and they feel got at and hard done by. But if you have a routine – at this time in the day, at this point in what we're doing, we do THIS – there is no argument. It's what we do. Full stop.

It helps with consistency

Children may sometimes like a surprise and something different, but on the whole they really crave and need consistency. They need to know this action brings forth that response and this bit of behaviour has that consequence. A routine and a structure reinforces that you, and life, have an important, underlying consistency.

Routines encourage children to co-operate, with each other and with you.

When children know what is expected they can work together instead of vying for attention or supremacy. Siblings who might otherwise be fighting could instead co-operate to get their tasks done.

It keeps them healthy and wise

When children go to bed on time and get up on time they have enough sleep to stay in good health and a good mood. Children with a sleep deficit have difficulties learning and indeed enjoying. It's no fun feeling below par all the time. Constant conflict in a family (and poor grades at school) may well be traced back to poor sleep.

It helps them anticipate the future instead of living only in the present

A routine can give children an awareness of future benefits against present demands. In other words, to accept we need to clean up and settle down now, but will play again in the afternoon, or tomorrow.

It helps you resist demands

If you have a routine it's so much easier not to give in to their demands to watch one more TV programme or DVD, or stay up that little bit later. It can be tempting, to stop the whining, but if you give in, 'just this once' it means you'll have the same fight again and again. Establish a routine and keep to it, and your children will know you mean it.

How to ask your child to do something and have them pay attention

It's easy to get into an oppositional situation with children. We frequently throw requests, or orders, at them on the run and when they ignore us or talk back we soon find ourselves spiralling into argument. There is a technique you can use whenever you want your child to listen to you and do as you ask that really works. It can take a bit of time and getting used to. It does require a bit more from you, in time and effort, than doing it the way you might be doing now. Trust me, it works and saves time in the long run.

Imagine this scenario: you are getting a meal ready. Your child is in the living room watching TV, or playing or drawing or whatever, as you prepare. The evening meal will be ready in ten minutes and on past experience you're about to begin the evening row. You'll call, your child will ignore you. You'll call again and this time they'll yell they want to see the end of the programme or finish whatever they are doing. You say it's ready and they shout back. You storm next door to say the meal is getting cold. Your child flounces to their bedroom in a fit of temper. They finally come to eat, sniffling and sulking, and you eat in a tense silence.

A STRATEGY THAT HELPS YOU BOTH AGREE

Before you begin cooking, go next door, crouch down to the level of your child, touch them on knee or arm and say their name and wait until you establish eye contact. This makes sure you and your child are communicating face to face – a great improvement on shouting through a door. It shows respect and a willingness to listen, and means the child in turn hears what you say and attends. Then say 'I'm about to cook. Want to come and chat with me? Food will be ready in 20 minutes.' Then, ask your child to repeat back to you what you've asked – 'Are we clear?' You could, if they don't repeat it back to you at once, say 'What are we doing?' When they do so, thank them.

If the child says they want to go on playing or watching TV or whatever, thank them for asking and say 'That's fine. Food will be on the table in 20 minutes. Will you be ready then?' You may then need to agree delaying a few minutes, or for them to make sure they can record or stream the programme for later, or find a convenient point to pause it. They may, given a direct invitation, be more willing to come into the kitchen and help you or chat with you – in which case, job done.

Check back every five minutes with a countdown. Go in, repeat the crouching down, touching, naming and eye contact and say 'Fifteen minutes – OK?' 'Ten minutes – hungry?' Then 'Five minutes – go and wash your hands.' Again, use descriptive praise to thank the child when they do as asked. Keep the contact eye to eye – remember to use the child's name, and a touch on the shoulder, arm or knee to make that connection. When it's zero, if the child has not come running, go in, say their name again, give them a hug and say 'Food!!'. If the child has been grumpy, be sympathetic 'You must be hungry – come and eat!' If the child won't come, go and eat and ignore them – don't be drawn in to an argument. By keeping the connection, being upbeat and calm, the chances are even an angry and upset child will join you. And again, always thank the child with descriptive praise when they comply 'You washed your hands and came to the table as asked – thank you!'

Remember the key points:

- ▶ Be in the same room, next to them.
- ▶ Use their name.
- ▶ Establish physical contact, and eye contact.
- ▶ State what you want, clearly.
- ▶ Ask for it to be repeated back to you so you know it's been heard and understood.
- ▶ Repeat at intervals.

Above all, thank each time you are heeded with descriptive praise.

It feels clumsy and artificial and awkward at first. After a few repetitions, and successes, you'll see how useful is this way of doing things.

Insight

It was 20 minutes until Christmas dinner but instead of telling my six-year-old granddaughter to get ready, I asked her to pass the message on to her grandfather. At 15, 10 and 5 minutes she delighted in being the one to go and remind him they needed to finish their game, then tidy it up, then go and wash their hands together. That it meant she was prepared and on time was by the by – she'd had great fun being the one to keep him on track, and to be in charge.

BEING FIRM

I have emphasized happiness as such an important concept, and it is a vital component in the wellbeing of you and your family. But that doesn't mean to say you should expect or even strive to make your children happy all the time. You can't. Rather than wanting them to be happy all the time or have no problems, it's more useful to help them to develop the ability to handle the ups and downs of life and weather the setbacks. It's the ability to enjoy the ups and cope with the downs without falling apart that will be their most important skill. And that means as well as playing with them and encouraging them, sometimes we say no to them.

SAYING NO

It used to be said that 'Spare the rod and spoil the child.' Thank goodness such harsh and punitive attitudes have been shown to be wrong. But for some parents it would seem that the pendulum has swung too far the other way. It's clear that in many cases parents are terrified to tell a child when they are behaving badly, for fear that putting your foot down causes lasting psychological damage. We seem to be a generation of parents pussyfooting around, treading on eggshells, rather than distress a child and court tears and complaints. So let's get one thing straight. Negligence and cruelty, regular criticism with no balancing praise, frequent inconsistency – those are damaging. Telling off a child who has done something they know is wrong, or firmly correcting one who is behaving in ways you know is antisocial, is not. Indeed, being hands-off and scared of saying 'No' causes as much damage as persistent punishment. It tells children you are frightened to maintain boundaries, to hold them to account and enforce good behaviour. In effect, you tell them your feelings are far more important to you than their wellbeing. That is not a comfortable message to hear as a child.

IT'S NOT GOING TO KILL YOUR CHILD TO BE TOLD OFF

Children who are constantly criticized, marginalized or neglected will obviously suffer. But that's no reason to feel you must never, ever cause your child a moment of unhappiness. The whole tenor of this book is how to maximize your child's and thus your family's happiness. But you don't do that by going out of your way to never ever be the source of dissatisfaction on their part. There will be appropriate moments when you have to say no, when you have to say don't, when you have to say you can't have or can't do. And of course that's going to produce wails, arguments, sulks and disagreement. And that may make you feel guilty or scared. As the adult it's your job to be able to judge when a moment of unhappiness is the cost of a later, better outcome.

USING THE CAT

CAT is a technique that builds on the ACT strategy – Adult, Child and Tools. This time, we start with the child and it's most useful when we need to get across to a child who is doing something we don't want. Let's take as an example two children running about playing in the house when we are trying to make a meal.

C – we use Child, to connect to the child by recognizing how they might feel and see it. So – 'I can see you're having a good time running around inside and don't want to go outside because it's raining'.

A – We explain our feelings. So – 'I'm worried all this play is going to knock something over and break it and that's stopping me concentrating on getting a meal fixed. I want you to stop running around indoors.'

T – We look for a tool to find a solution. So – 'You could come and help me cook. Or go outside and have fun getting wet. Or play something quiet indoors like a board game, or do some craftwork. Which is it to be?'

By recognizing and acknowledging the child's feelings you get alongside rather than in opposition with them. By explaining your own feelings you don't blame them but own the problem – it is, after all, your problem not theirs – and ask them to recognize your feelings. You then come up with a solution that works for you, but open the door to them suggesting other ones that might also work – such as using the time before the meal to do their homework.

CHILDREN FEEL STRESS TOO

Children are like barometers. They pick up and display the emotional atmosphere in their family and the world around them. You may think they won't notice and can't understand any of the problems you are having. And you may be right about their not understanding what it is all about, but they can certainly notice tension and unhappiness, and broadcast it as their own. Family disputes, family loss, family unhappiness will all affect a child and make them unhappy and stressed. And they can have their own problems too. Even very young children can feel the pressure of expectations and the misery of conflict with friends. We may find it difficult to recognize or say 'I'm feeling miserable or getting headaches because my partner and I are going through a bad patch in our relationship'. Children, with even less experience of life, are even worse than we are at being able to pinpoint the source of their misery. What they will often do is show it. Stress may leak out as:

▶ Stomach aches
▶ Headaches

- ▸ General aches and pains
- ▸ Teeth grinding
- ▸ Sleep problems

Or the child may:

- ▸ Wet the bed
- ▸ Be weepy and clingy
- ▸ Be irritable
- ▸ Be anxious
- ▸ Put themselves down a lot

We need to recognize the signs of stress, and respond appropriately. Children showing stress may need you to deal with your own first, so you can show a good example by taking measures to change, and so you are no longer putting them on edge with your distress. Then, they may need you to give them extra time, to hug and kiss, to read together and play, to talk over anything that is worrying them. You may need to be a detective asking yourself when this behaviour began and what happened around that time, to find the cause of it. It's often the cause that needs to be addressed in order for the behaviour to be tackled.

TIME OUTS

The Time Out technique has become popular, since it's often shown in parenting programmes on TV. To be effective, Time Outs need to be:

- ▸ Only used when absolutely necessary
- ▸ Used with care and for short periods
- ▸ Used as an opportunity for reflection, and with explanation

It's a last resort mechanism and in effect it's an extreme form of ignoring a child's bad behaviour, and of removing them from you for a few minutes so they can calm down and so can you. But it also needs to be a time for your child to recognize what they've done that you don't like, and to agree to act differently. Think of it like that and you will find it effective.

STICKER CHARTS

This is another technique that many people try – it can be stunningly effective, if used properly. If you have something you and your child are struggling with – getting up in the morning, brushing hair or cleaning teeth – you can set up a sticker chart to encourage the behaviour you want.

How do you do it?

Tell the child, very clearly, what it is you want them to do. Make or buy a calendar or wall chart, a supply of gold star stickers, and a supply of sad faces (dots you can make into frowning faces.) Explain every time they do what you've asked you will award them a gold star. Every time they don't, they'll get a frowny face. Show them the chart – one star for every day the task is done without complaint. To begin with, say for every five consecutive stars they can have a treat. Discuss the treat they'd like. Sweets or chocolate are not a good idea – make the treats a special game or visit or extra story read at bedtime. When they're doing five, move it to six then seven.

Sticker charts work if:

▶ You are specific
▶ You do need to be very clear what it is you want, and don't want.
▶ You persist

It can feel very boring and quite frustrating, when the child is struggling. If it's not working, you may need to examine exactly what is going on and why. Why is the child having such a problem with this task, or why they have decided to make it such a point of conflict. Talking this over with someone objective could help you put your finger on the problem.

You keep to the rules

Having explained and set up the sticker chart it's really important that you do what you have said. This means withholding a gold star on the days when the child has not earned one, and ignoring whines and wails when the end of the week comes and no treat has been deserved. Children don't learn if they don't recognize consequences.

WHAT DOESN'T HELP?

Most of us have been guilty of lashing out at times – at an object when we trip over it and it gets in the way, at the dog for getting under your feet one more time…and at a child for pushing our buttons just once too often. I'd argue that happiness and smacking don't really go together. Smacking might be defended if the result of a short, sharp physical punishment once in a while resulted in good behaviour and agreement, peace and serenity reigning the rest of the time. Sadly, both our own experience and research shows it does not. Families that smack find they go on smacking. When we look at the punishment books schools used to keep recording who received corporal punishment, we find an interesting situation. Surely, if it worked as a deterrent or a way of training a child to know wrong from right, children who had been punished would not need to be punished again? Far from smacking being an effective way of teaching a child not to behave badly, the same children come up again and again.

Similarly, families who smack find physical punishment tends to lead to more physical punishment. Because, above all, it doesn't work. People who defend it says it does – 'I was smacked and it never did me any harm.' 'I was smacked and it taught me wrong from right.' 'I was smacked and I never did that again.' I think we always edit our memories to fit in with the story we think is right. And we always forgive and love our parents, so if they did it, it's hard to say 'My parents were wrong and I wish they hadn't done that.' We defend them, copy them and then defend ourselves.

Smacking:

Hurts

Children look to us for protection and comfort. It can be highly confusing for a young child to have the people they look to for security and safety actually handing out pain and discomfort.

Doesn't teach what you're trying to say

Children feel the pain but very rarely make a clear association between the punishment and the behaviour that led to it. They think 'Mum/Dad was angry with me' not 'I did so-and-so and mustn't do it again.'

Teaches might is right

What they do learn, rapidly, is that using force is fine. You give them a first-class example to model themselves on with their peers, or with smaller children.

Frightens and confuses them

The reality is that we usually hit because we react. We've told them not to do something and they push the limits one more time. Or we're having a bad day and something they do is the final straw. Or someone or something else winds us up and they happen to say or do something at just the wrong time. They get the rough end of it, and they know it's unjust.

SO WHAT SHOULD YOU DO INSTEAD?

Avoiding smacking may need a change of mindset. It may need you to accept that while your parents did their best and loved you, their actions were not the ones you want to follow. The trick is to move from negative parenting – where you notice and punish wrongdoing – to positive parenting – where you notice and praise doing right. It also means taking responsibility for both teaching children and guiding them before behaviour you might not want occurs.

POSITIVE PARENTING

Positive parenting takes time, patience and effort. The carrot is that it saves time, patience and effort in the long run. Let's take the example of a shopping trip with a child as the experience when we often feel our children act up and make it all so much harder. Children probably get shouted at or smacked more often before, during or after a shopping trip than at any other time. So how do we make sure that is not what we need to make the experience acceptable? We've dealt briefly with managing when it's a toddler – how do we extend that to an older child?

What often happens is that we rush around getting ready – getting together a shopping list, turning of the kettle, collecting bags and clothing and finally telling our child we're off.

Pinch Point One: child objects – they want to go on painting, playing, watching TV. There's a struggle to get them ready, against their sulks and arguments. By the time we're on our way, we're both flustered and frazzled.

We get to the supermarket and tell the child we don't want a repeat of last time when they ran up and down the aisles and asked for crisps. 'Behave this time!' we say.

Pinch Point two: child runs up and down the aisles and asks for crisps. Child trails behind us, bored, asks incessant questions, and when we finally get to the payout, fingers the sweets there and whines for them, and gets in the way when we're trying to pack bags, reaching for biscuits and other brightly coloured packets.

We feel everybody in the shop is glaring at us, criticizing our parenting skills and thinking 'What that child needs is a good spanking/telling off!'

Pinch Point Three: even though we know it's going to result in more crying, we smack or shout, because not to do so we feel makes us look like a bad parent.

Child goes into major sulk and digs heels in.

Pinch Point Four: we feel utterly powerless and out of control, and increasingly frustrated, trying to deal with child and handle a trolley full of shopping. We might walk away – child becomes even more argumentative. We might try to hustle child out of the supermarket – child struggles, and redoubles efforts. We might manhandle child into the car, and child goes totally all out into meltdown, and we feel terrible.

Back home feeling tired, grumpy and hungry – and that's us, let alone how the child feels and lets us know they feel through tears, a strop or a continuing full blown shouting match.

Pinch Point Five: we're both exhausted, and we're wondering whether we can ever do that again – and knowing shopping has to be done so the answer may well be yes.

So how can we avoid all those pinch points, or at least negotiate our way round them, in future?

Pinch Point One: child wants to go on doing what they're doing.

You'd be pretty fed up too if your partner made a habit of suddenly turning up by your side and hustling you out the door to do something they had planned, but not told you about. We may think young children should notice and know when we're going out. And indeed, we may have said so at some point beforehand. But do we make an effort to really clue them into our plans, and prepare them? They need to know 'We're going shopping.' Children need updates and reminders. 'Don't forget, we're going shopping soon...' They need us to take responsibility for timekeeping, so that we monitor when they begin a game or a session of painting or watching TV, and ensure it can be finished and put aside when we need to go. They need a countdown, so we tell them 15, 10 and 5 minutes before we want to get ready so they're prepared to do so as well. With younger children a challenge 'Can you get the toys put away/your things together/your shoes on as quickly as me?' or a choice 'Blue shoes or red?' always helps. With older children often a simple 'Shoes on!' suffices.

Pinch Point Two: we don't want a repeat of former bad behaviour.

There are three strategies to stop running around and pester power. *First* is that you have to ask for what you want, not what you don't want. When you tell a child 'Don't run in the aisles and ask for sweets' all the child hears is 'Run in the aisles' and 'Sweets.' You couldn't programme them better to make both your lives miserable. Instead, say what you DO want. 'I'd like you to stay by me. Please stay by me, hold my hand or hold on to the trolley.'

The *second* is to list and enlist. Give your child a task. There are reasons they run around. One is boredom – shopping is not exactly a first choice for a child as a fun way of spending an hour (it may not be yours, either!) so of course they liven it up with some activity. So give them some. Harness the other reason they grab stuff off shelves – they're copying you. You do it so they want to get into the act. And to be helpful and win your approval. It's often very disheartening when their efforts to be so supportive are treated with disdain. Give them a choice – 'Will you hold the list and cross things off as I say, or shall I hold the list and you fetch stuff?' And yes, it will take longer – you have to be patient and let them struggle to pick items up and put them in the trolley. It will take less time than a tantrum, believe me. Encourage them to help you take things out of the trolley onto the checkout, or pack items away when they've gone through. Again, it will take time. I've never been at a checkout when a parent has been doing this where other people were anything but charmed, impressed and patient.

Third, discuss a reward. It's best to do this beforehand, and it's also best if this is not sweets or crisps or other food, but time. Agree when you have finished your tasks, if they have done as you asked, you will make something or play something together with them; take them to run around in the park; you or the other parent will read an extra bedtime story. You'll have saved the time needed to allow them some quality play or quiet time with you with the time you've saved not arguing!

Pinch Point Three: don't let your worry over other people's reactions push you into doing something that is not right for you or your child.

You may be right that people are judging you and wishing you would apply a firm hand. If you and your partner were disagreeing in public and someone felt the right thing for one of you to do was punch the other would that be a good reason to do it? I wish more people would do what I always do in such circumstances – catch the parent's eye, make a sympathetic face and say 'It's tough being a parent sometimes, isn't it?' Sympathy and a kind word can help and if no-one around you is prepared to show it, show it to yourself and your child.

Pinch Point Four: if your child does kick off, take a deep breath and slow down.

Your tension and upset increases the stress. Children erupt when they become overwhelmed with their feelings. Imagine your child like a cup. Usually, rational thought and emotions balance each other out. When they have a tantrum it's because the cup has become flooded with feelings, drowning out the rational thought. The child becomes literally incapable of thinking their way past the powerful feelings they are having. And that's scary. What might have begun as a protest, some frustration and confusion and a bit of anger and maybe some jealousy or longing for a treat or some attention, suddenly becomes panic. The child can be overcome with the strength of what they are experiencing, and unable to come down from it. Sometimes the best way to deal with a really upset child is to hold them lovingly and firmly – often, getting behind them and crouching or sitting down enfolding them in your arms – and soothing them until the whole thing recedes. You may need to ask a shop assistant to look after your shopping, or if it's before the checkout, simply abandon it.

Pinch Point Five: Tired and hungry

If you've tried the previous suggestions this time you may not be quite as exhausted as usual. Whatever, aim to restore both your and your child's energy levels as soon as you get out of the shop, or walk in the door. A drink and a snack take priority to driving home, or unpacking shopping and putting it away. Then attend to the reward if the child has done as you've asked, or regretful explanation as to why child must do better next time. It's important to give rewards when earned and equally important to withhold them, with a clear description of what they did you don't want repeating and what you'd like next time. Then, debrief yourself. What worked, what did not? What might you do differently next time?

THE ULTIMATE SANCTION

If you're stuck in a repeating pattern with a child who won't listen or do as you've asked, go for the ultimate sanction. Get a friend or relative you trust to mind the child when you go shopping, and make it absolutely clear the time with them is not to be a reward. You'll hardly be getting your point across if they have a wonderful time being spoiled and pampered. Agree that the child can paint or play but no TV and no special games. What you want to establish is that you are upset and disappointed and prepared to make going shopping more fun, but you need them to do their part and co-operate. Don't reward them if they don't do as asked, but give them a chance to calm down and reflect in a quiet time on what they could do to co-operate. Children always want your acceptance and appreciation and as long as you can give them a clear explanation of what you want, will usually do it. You may think that being let off the chore of coming shopping with you would be a relief. In fact, they'll feel left out and rejected. Especially if you emphasize what you might have done with them afterwards as the treat if they had come and behaved.

Insight

Always tell children what you want, not what you don't want. The clearer you are on your request, the more likely they are to please you.

Sibling rivalry

If you have more than one child, sometime or other you're going to have trouble. If you think children will never feel rivalry, or you believe your children have never felt like rivals, or remember your childhood as perfectly peaceful…take off those blinkers! Because while we can certainly do a lot to prevent fighting and bring down the level of conflict, and indeed broker good and caring as well as loving relationships between our children, the feelings of rivalry are natural, normal, common and indeed inevitable.

Just think for a moment how it feels to a child when a brother or sister comes along. Put yourself in the picture. Your partner bounces up to you one day and tells you, with every evidence of joy, that they love you so much they're going to get another partner. The new arrival will live with you and share the time they spend with you and the love they have for you. Won't that be fun? And of course you won't mind supervising the new arrival, helping them learn the ropes and sharing your toys and games. And maybe some of your cast off clothes – they could go to the new arrival as of course you don't need them now. How would you feel?

KNOCKED OFF THE THRONE

Older children feel supplanted. There they were, the king or queen of your heart, on their solitary throne commanding your full attention. Along comes the pretender and pushes them off that throne. From early days, even before the baby appears, focus is on them and even if children can accept you love them as much, they are right in feeling you have to share your time and consideration – and this rankles.

As for the new arrival, once they can recognize what there is in their environment, there is the incumbent: bigger, faster, more knowledgeable and there first. They may feel forever in the shadow of their sibling, struggling to catch up and keep up. No wonder they feel competitive, and challenged.

Given this, you can see and understand why children may be primed to be in contention and in conflict. However, you have one asset going for you, and them. This is that although they may feel in competition for your attention, they are also united in the same desire – to be approved of by you. They are on the same team, and since each of them is also a part of you, they also see each other as allies. However much they might tend to squabble when together, separate siblings and you're likely to get them clamouring to be allowed back together. Your task is to maximize the tendency to want to be together and co-operating, and minimize the tendency to be at war.

HOW TO PREVENT SIBLINGS FIGHTING

There are plenty of things you can do to set the scene for siblings to co-operate. It helps if you have these in mind before the event – before a second child is on the way. But if you miss the boat, don't despair – you can change things even when you have an existing situation.

We've talked already about what you can do beforehand to prepare a child for the arrival of a newcomer. What can you do once both are up and around, and able to communicate?

From the beginning, make sure you give each child individual attention, as well as shared time. Older children particularly will feel the younger is privileged, because at first, being small and helpless, you have to do so much for and with them. You may not, reasonably, be able to give a toddler or child equal time to a baby. But you can make a point of giving special time, when the baby is sleeping or with the other parent or another adult. Emphasizing how precious is the time you share with them playing, and going through the bedtime routine, can go a long way to evening it up.

Asking them to co-operate and share from a young age may be frustrating because young children are naturally selfish – they have to be taught and to learn these skills. Your elder child may feel it more than annoying if they're ready to share and the younger isn't. Explain to, support and mollify the elder child while training the younger to learn those skills.

Never compare children. You'll be setting them up to battle if you ever say anything that resembles 'Look at your big/little brother – they can do it!' Praise and congratulate each for their own trials and struggles. Don't make comparisons.

Give them space and respect both territory and belongings. They might have to share a room. You might feel it makes sense to share toys. Children will keenly feel invaded. Set up a shared room with separate areas and enforce the rule that says they don't cross boundaries, and don't touch belongings, without invitation. Some games and toys, just as other areas of the house, will be common ground. Make it clear which these are. They're more likely to co-operate and share those if they can feel there is respect for their own.

Recognize the touch-paper times – moments when kids are primed to explode, and you might want to step in and separate them before it happens. Coming home from school might be one, when all kids can be tired and hungry and so cranky. Make a point of saying no interaction until you can get them home, fed, paid attention to and rested.

Don't put older children in a position of responsibility over younger ones until they can recognize when it's appropriate and when it is not. Asking a teenager to watch a child while you go to the shops is understandable. But the situation you do not want to encourage is where one child starts telling another what to do with the authority of an adult – often, standing behind you while you're reading the riot act and adding their two penny's worth with satisfaction at the discomfort of the younger. That only tends to infuriate the younger. If you have Family Rules and everyone can quote them, that's fine. But it's your job to be responsible, not a child, and you can remind them by saying 'Thank you darling. I'm glad you know the family rules but it's my job to be in charge.'

Teach your children to negotiate and aim for a win/win deal. Win/lose is when one person comes out on top and the other gets nothing. Lose/lose is often the result of sibling fights – you step in and take the toy or treat away altogether. What they want to go for is a situation where both get at least part of what they want. So show them how to say 'What do we want? How can we make sure both of us get some of that?' You can suggest taking turns, when it's a toy or game. Or trading – if we play my game first then I'll play yours. You can teach them to divide up a treat, if it's food for instance. THE rule is one cuts or divvies up, and the other chooses – that is the gold standard for ensuring fairness!

Be a model for and enforce the rule of respect. Say 'In this family we don't badmouth anyone – we don't swear at people, say unkind things, call them names or be mean.' Show this yourself – don't use disrespect in disagreements with your partner or badmouth anyone else. That may be hard the next time someone cuts you up or bumps into you. Take a deep breath and think of the example you're giving. Being so good will give you a glow of satisfaction that being nasty cannot.

Set up a treats jar. Explain that every time they are kind, co-operative and play without fighting or do something nice for each other you'll put a penny in the jar. Every time you see them fighting, being unkind, refusing to share, you'll take a penny out. When the jar is full you'll use the money to take them on a really special treat.

Discuss sanctions with your partner so you can be singing from the same song-sheet, and indeed when your children get a bit older, with them. Punishment tends to backfire. Smacking is counterproductive but so is shouting or taking away privileges.

Being punished tends to make children feel resentful. They often don't remember what it was they did wrong, but concentrate on being angry at you, and their sibling. What does work is positive discipline, where you praise and notice good behaviour and tend to ignore the minor infractions. What can also be effective with sibling fights is restorative justice, when the aggressor does something to make up for their behaviour, or when both warring kids repair the breach.

Teach your children that it's OK to have bad feelings – we all do – but it's not OK to act on them. Help them by putting it into words. So: 'I can see that you're angry with your sister. You can tell her how you feel in words. But in this family, we don't hit.' Or 'I can see you're upset that your brother stays up half an hour later than you. When you're his age, you can too. But for now you go to bed at this time. You can say you're jealous but you don't break her things or shout at me.' Reinforce 'Say it in words, not in actions.'

Help your children find other ways to show feelings than hitting out. Anger management is recognizing feelings, accepting them and then discharging them safely. You could make a game of it – how many ways can we find to work off anger? Draw it, paint it, write the words, make the words with magnetic letters, dance to music, run around outside, hit pillows, throw a ball against a wall.

Insight

Sometimes, you just need to wait ten minutes. Children can erupt in total fury at a sibling and be in a screaming fight, saying they hate each other, and a few minutes later be playing perfectly happily. You're still traumatized – they've forgotten the whole thing. Children live in the moment while we, as adults, tend to hold states of mind, and emotions, for some time. It helps sometimes to simply manage the immediate crisis because it may quickly blow over.

You can also teach even small children conflict management. Ask them to join you in working out ways of not arguing. What should you do if you disagree? How about saying 'You feel this, I feel that, how can we agree?' Or agreeing to staying nice and saying what you think without calling each other names. What should you do if you see someone else is getting angry? How about suggesting a time out until you both calm down, or asking a grown up to help?

Model anger management and conflict resolution yourselves. When you and your partner have a disagreement, show your children how you keep your temper and talk it through.

Help your children learn how to sympathize, and empathize. Don't expect them to manage these at first – it takes time and development to do so. But you can speed this along by pointing out 'He's crying. He must feel sad. Shall we help?' 'I think your sister is really angry. Shall we find out why?' If you spring to help a child who is hurt or distressed, when the crisis is over you can invite the other child to join in. 'Shall we see what we can do to make him feel better?'

Make saying nice things to and about each other a family tradition and game. You could introduce it as a mealtime sport – you go round the table so everyone takes the opportunity to come up with something nice they'd like to say to everyone else. 'Thank you Dad for playing with me' 'Thank you Jane for letting me have a go with your game' 'Thank you Mum for making my favourite meal'.

Make allowances. They're learning and can't be expected to take all the lessons at once. It's dispiriting for them if you expect too much, too early, and doesn't actually make them feel they must do better if they always feel they get it wrong. Repeat the message, tell them you have full confidence they will do better next time.

WHAT DO YOU DO IF THEY DO FIGHT?

To a certain extent, children need to learn how to settle their own fights. One reason is that often you don't and can't know who started it, what happened and why. By intervening you could be reinforcing bad behaviour and breeding resentment by supporting the aggressor against the victim. But you do need to keep an eye on what is going on, and use the quiet bedtime chat to check out all is well. Otherwise, whether you like it or not, bullying may be going on – and that's not always the larger and stronger who's victimizing the smaller and weaker. But if you've instilled all the ideas already mentioned, they may still go head to head but use the skills to settle it in a reasonable manner.

If one child is hurt, concentrate on them, not the one who caused the hurt. If your first action is to tell the aggressor off, you are in effect rewarding them: they hit out and then get all the attention. Stem the tears, patch up wounds, restore calm. Then, take the next step.

Don't take sides or try to sort out who did what. Your task is to stop conflict and get them to come to an agreement. Remind them 'We don't hit or call people names in this family.' Ask them if they can work this out, or go back to playing together, or need time to cool off.

If emotions are running high, or they request it, ask everyone to agree to a ten-minute break to calm down and cool off. Separate them, but it's better to have them back to back in the same room than sent to their rooms. Ask them to read, draw, paint or quietly play.

When they're ready, bring them back together. Explain a coin is being taken out of the jar and another will go unless they can make up. The rule is that you want to know what happened, but don't want to hear accusations. It's not about telling tales – although if the other child did something dangerous they need to tell you. What you need to hear is 'We...': 'We wanted to play a game and we both wanted to go first.' 'We wanted to watch a programme but couldn't agree which one' Or, they might say honestly 'He wanted to play with my toy and I didn't want to share.' Each can have an opportunity to say how they feel and what they want the other one to know. But, it is about their feelings – I feel hurt, I feel angry, I feel ignored – not about what they think the other person did. Toss a coin to choose who goes first then get each to tell the other how they feel and what they would like now. Ask each child to say what they understood their sibling to have felt – that builds empathy and understanding. Help them come up with a plan for now, and a plan for if this happens again.

What are your priorities? Apparently, studies show that towards the end of their lives people often look back with regret and realize they paid more attention to less important aspects of their lives. Nobody says on their deathbed that they wished they'd spent more time at the office – yet many say they wish they'd spent more time and gave more attention to family and friends. Look at the things you spend time and effort on, and work out:

▶ Which you'll look back at and wish you'd done more. What could you do now to make sure you don't have such regrets?
▶ Which you'll look back at and realize weren't as important as you'd thought. What could you do now to make them less of a priority?

KEY POINTS

1 As your toddler becomes a child, communication becomes easier and 'It's good to talk' – listening and talking to your child as much as possible – becomes the ideal for happy parenting.

2 Unqualified praise for a child's every effort does not necessarily help them learn about life. Helping children learn from their failures can be far more realistic.

3 Learn the lessons of 'Fill your cup.' You cannot look after others successfully if you don't look after yourself.

4 If you are returning to your family after being away all day, make sure it is 'Family first.' Getting together again should be far more important than rushing to deal with distractions like e-mails or messages.

5 Having made your child an active and contributing part of the family, go in for regular Family Round Table meetings where everyone, including the youngest, can discuss things together and have their say.

6 Like any organization, the family should have rules that are agreed and observed by everyone. Use your Family Round Table to establish these to everyone's satisfaction.

7 Allocating and doing chores is a core part of a child's and family's growing up together.

8 Similarly, the making and observance of routines gives everyone a feeling of security within a structured family framework.

9 Now is the time – with increased mutual communication – to change the ACT technique of toddler days to the CAT (Child, Adult, Tools) approach to childhood. This will put you alongside rather than in opposition to your child.

10 Say 'Yes' to Positive Parenting. It may take more time, patience and effort at the moment, but will save you all of these things in the long run.

BEING HAPPY

How are you doing with the fun sheet? Here are a few more ideas to add – do your own!

Small things	Medium things	Big things
Bake a cake with your child. Lie on the floor with your children and pretend to be kittens. Walk the dog, play with the cat. Smile at and say 'Hi!' to a neighbour.	Get a new book to read your child. Play a board game. Go to a car boot sale. Have a tea party. Try cooking a new dish and find it works.	Have a family picnic – even if it's in winter, in the rain, in the car. Visit a National Trust home. Go on a chocolate factory tour. Watch a Civil War re-enactment. Go for a long walk in the country.

5

....

The teenager

In this chapter you will learn:
- *That teenagers have an important developmental task, and it's to separate from their parents*
- *That friends now assume prime position in their lives, but they still want and need shared family time*
- *The importance of 'I' statements*
- *To encourage your teenagers to sort out their own problems*

Having a happy family life so often depends on your getting the balance right between guiding your children firmly and listening to their needs, wishes and opinions keenly. How you help and support your child to grow from a small child to a reasoning adult and to do so as someone who is kind and caring, empathetic and sympathetic, and a socialized being, is really a process. In many cases the foundations behind the skills you use and the strategies you adopt to teach them and communicate with them are the same whether it's a baby or a teenager.

Step changes

But there are two step changes – times when it's not just about being flexible and making small, gradual changes as they grow, but two transitions where you have to recognize you are in a whole different game. One is when you move from parenting a baby to a toddler. The fundamentals of dealing with a baby, and dealing with a toddler, have a quite obvious difference – with the first you do your best to be in close contact and respond to their needs, while with the latter you begin to introduce the concept that they are not the centre of the universe, must sometimes wait and that certain limits and boundaries have come into play.

With teenagers there is another lurch sideways. You are the most important person in your child's life, the person they look to and look up to. What they want most of all is your approval and to be in close connection with you, and your main role is to guide and direct. But a teenager, while still loving you, needing you and your approval and looking up to you, requires most of all to separate and stand on their own two feet. This may lead them to reject you and your ideas and mores, to be careless about your feelings, to respect the opinions of friends and other adults more than yours and to be defiant and rebellious. It really can feel as if, overnight, a different being has come to stay.

Teenagers want control of their own lives

Teenagers are rebellious, opinionated, idealistic and either totally loudmouthed or utterly monosyllabic. And it's one of life's bitter jokes that, at the same time as children go through their most difficult, angst-ridden period of adolescence, their parents may be entering the midlife crisis. It's the collision of birthdays with os and 5s at the end – 40 and 15 being perhaps the most explosive – that often causes the most painful misunderstandings. Stroppy teenagers struggling to take some control over their lives clash head on with adults who are beginning to wonder, 'Is this all there is?' Young teens contend with physical changes that leave them awkward and clumsy, and older teens agonize over the emotional changes that have them demanding independence while still craving care and security. At the same time, parents might be struggling with emotional issues and financial and work related problems, as well as their own version of physical changes that leave them feeling less than satisfied with themselves.

YOUR APPROVAL IS STILL VALUED

Parents can feel rejected and judged and may either suggest or give in to demands from teenagers for them to be left alone in their own rooms, for peace and quiet or a release from tension and strife. However, while giving them privacy at times, this is the time when it may be most important to insist on shared family time as well. Teenagers may seem to have rejected their parents, but parents' approval is still key to their wellbeing and self-worth. Even if you haven't laid the ground work earlier for family meetings and discussions, now is the time to reinstate it or create it and hold to it. Family Round Table discussions will help all of you deal with disagreements or conflict. You do need to insist, and make a space in the family diary, for these to be convened at least once a week, with everyone having the right to call an extra one at any time if there are problems that need thrashing out.

But equally, informal and regular time together is vital. This is one of the reasons I would say that there are two issues which should be sacrosanct and no argument. One is eating together. The other is no media in bedrooms.

SHARED MEALS

Eating together is such a vital part of family life, and one that seems to have gone by the board in many families. We all live busy lives – not just parents but children too, with schoolwork jostling with after-school activities and keeping up social contacts. In so many families it's really hard to manage everyone's timetables so that the family can be at home to eat together around a table. It's difficult when children are in primary school and often felt to be impossible when they are teenagers. What so often happens is that people eat on the run or from plates on their lap while watching a screen, from meals heated up in a microwave or quickly put together.

But eating together is so very important. It's actually something we should prioritize and make happen – we should cancel other activities and commitments in favour of regular meals. Why? Because it's the key to communication. It's the chance to chat together in a non-confrontational way with everyone sharing ideas and having fun. If your experience is that mealtimes are a time of argument and conflict that's probably because it's the only opportunity you make to share time. Make Family Round Tables or private discussions the moments to bring contentious issues. Ban rows at mealtimes and make breaking bread together something you can all enjoy – a haven and moment of peace and accord and pleasure.

To have the best experience you should:

▶ Make food from scratch, and invite your children and partner to help you make it. It's not a chore – it's an opportunity to have an input in what you'll be eating, and to start off the chat in the kitchen.

▶ Ban rows – if there are any issues say 'Let's leave this for later – we will discuss it at a Family Round table'.
▶ Resist impulses to criticize eating habits, sitting habits, any habits – and ask your children not to do so against siblings. Simply enjoy being together with no carping.
▶ Come to the table with some ideas to get discussions going – see the end of this chapter. You could ask everyone to say three things that made them happy today, or three things they'd like to do tomorrow. Welcome their input.

NO ELECTRONICS IN BEDROOMS

The other factor that works so very much against happy family life is allowing children to have electronic media in their bedrooms. It's easy to see why this is felt to be advantageous. However, the disadvantages far, FAR outweigh the advantages. What are the pluses and minuses? Come up with your own but I would say the pluses might be:

▶ You can all watch what you want when you want it with no arguments.
▶ You can have the living room and some peace and quiet to yourself.
▶ Kids can study in peace.
▶ Young people can keep in touch with friends without bothering you.

What are the disadvantages?

▶ You have no control over what they may be doing – what they may be accessing, how often and how late.
▶ Electronic media is highly stimulating – it keeps children awake and can be accessed at any time.
▶ They don't need to learn how to negotiate and compromise.
▶ There is no family unity – everyone is in their own room, on their own.
▶ If children do get into trouble – experiencing cyber-bullying, accessing porn that disturbs them – they may find it hard to come to you for help as they feel it's their responsibility or fault.

You all want to use the media that is available. But would it not be better to do so as a family? Given that you can now stream, time shift and record, and that so many programmes repeat on the same channel or another one later in the week, there is never any excuse for anyone to miss something they really value. What may also be most valuable is the opportunity for the family to see programmes or games or anything together, to share it, discuss it, criticize it. And of course, to learn discussion, negotiation and compromise to achieve some happy medium.

Media in shared rooms

Making it a rule to have media in the shared spaces, whether living room, kitchen or a hallway, allows you several levels of essential control. You can and should allow your children some privacy and the right to chat to friends. But you also need to make it clear that certain behaviour is off limits. Accessing inappropriate websites, being unpleasant online, having contact with people who may prove to be dangerous are all things you as a parent need to and want to monitor and prevent. An understanding that you respect their privacy but reserve the right to pass by and look over their shoulder, is vital. So too is the agreement that hiding discussions or pages and clearing history is the trigger for being banned access for at least a month. It's so much easier to keep tabs if the media is in public rooms, even if you find some of the things they then watch or play with are noisy and a waste of your time. Better that then having them up in their bedrooms, hardly talking to you and watching porn, getting bullied or learning how to be a troll (someone who posts gratuitously nasty remarks online) or being groomed till 3 a.m. in the morning.

No computers!

So my rule is no computers of any sort – desktops, laptops, netbooks, tablets…none – in bedrooms. You can vary this if you have a child who really does need peace and quiet to do homework. Curiously, most prefer noise and bustle and would be fine to do it at the kitchen table or in a shared, public study area. But if you really do feel they can make a case, the rules may be on a non-internet-enabled machine – if they need to research they do it in the shared rooms. And you want to see their results after a session. And while they are upstairs, their mobiles are downstairs.

And of course, in bedrooms no television or games consoles, for the same reasons: flickering screens and stimulation keep them awake and can be accessed even when you have gone to bed and they should have. And no mobiles – these should be parked in the main room and turned off during family meals or other family times. Best practice is to agree times and a set amount of time in the evening when they can chat to people outside the house, and when you'd like them to be available to you. Over mealtimes, for instance, all of you should switch off.

Arguments will happen

Teenagers and parents will always argue, even when they love and respect and really, really want the best for each other. The problem is that teenagers have a job to do and so do parents, and they're incompatible. Parents need to protect, to guide and to care for their kids. Teenagers need to break free, to disconnect and to find their own personalities and opinions. If it's to work without too much shouting, slamming of doors and tears, both sides have to understand the other's viewpoint.

It's hard facing a teenager against whom you have very few sanctions – how do you make someone your height and size do anything they don't want to? The answer is, with strategies. You listen, you find out what's underneath the behaviour and sometimes you put your foot down.

BAD BEHAVIOUR

Teenagers don't behave badly simply for the fun of it. Bad behaviour is about bad feelings. Kids can't explain what they feel and so they react and act it out: anxiety, unhappiness or confusion become sulks and defiance. A teenager who feels they are falling behind with work and struggling at school often responds by insisting, 'This isn't for me – I want to leave!' rather than being able to say, 'Excuse me, I think I need some extra help.'

But given space and time, teenagers can be surprisingly insightful. It's not uncommon for them to find it hard to back down from their own mistakes but to support and encourage friends or younger siblings to do better.

Teenage years

Having a teenager is often seen as the most difficult part of being a parent. Parents often say they are not looking forward to it, and the media and other parents seem to delight in predicting doom and gloom for that stage of your family life. One minute into your child's thirteenth birthday and all will be rebellion and defiance, conflict and misery for the next seven years. At least. It's hardly a recipe for a happy family, is it? So how can we make this period not just tolerable, but fun?

KNOWING WHAT TEENS NEED

Children need to know that their parents are there for them – that there is a bond between them and that the parent will protect, care for and love them. When children are given positive, consistent nurture two things happen. One is that they can develop similar feelings and behaviour for other people – they can be loving, kind and supportive. The other is that they can separate at the appropriate time and look after themselves. Children in families that have undergone interruption or trauma – separated families, single families – can thrive as well as children in any other form of happy family, as long as the bonds and that certainty that their parents love them and are mindful of them remain.

The importance of the attachment work you have done while they were babies, toddlers and children can often be seen when children become adolescents, and start to pull away. Teenagers are apprentice adults and in order for them to become confident and competent in looking after themselves they need to rebel, to choose music, clothing, friends and even philosophies that distinguish them as far as possible from their parents. But the fact is that the stronger the attachment, the more confidence the teenager will have in being able to disconnect, knowing the parents will be there as a safety net. It's very similar to the fact that toddlers who feel safe, attached and loved can launch themselves away from the sheltering arms of a parent to learn to walk, knowing they can fall back on you when necessary. In a sense, the more rejecting they are, the more they respect and love you – they love and respect you enough to know you will love them, no matter what. And even if you look back and think you haven't done enough, it's never too late to connect and redress.

Insight

There is always a reason why people behave the way they do. It may seem out of character and out of proportion and you – and the person themselves – may have no idea what their actions are all about. But there is always a reason, even if it is difficult to understand and apparently has nothing to do with what is going on in the here and now.

BAD MOUTHING KIDS

A barrier is that it is easy, when teenagers become defiant and rebellious and often contrary and even rude, to respond in kind. Parents may find themselves falling into a critical mode where any discussion, with partners or friends, about our teenage children is a complaint or a condemnation and we can be very disparaging. We often do it because we're hurt and angry – after all, they started it first! But the problem is it can become entrenched and hard to get round. And even if we try to make an effort not to tell them directly how we feel, it leaks out in our tone and attitude towards them, or they overhear. Most of the time of course, we do it in front of them with the intention of letting them eavesdrop. When we find ourselves in conflict with our young people it helps to remember that it's the behaviour, not the teenager, we don't like – and that they are just doing what is normal for their age and development. A useful strategy to develop is that whenever we want to pick up on something they do that we don't like, describe the behaviour not the person. And, say what it does to you rather than what you think they are doing. What often goes wrong is that we put a label on the person, and a judgement. So:

> *'You left that mess for me to clear up! You're so lazy!'*

This leads to arguments because the young person will naturally insist they didn't mean to make work for you. But they will also feel at a dead end, because in labelling them you've told them that that's it, they're stuck in being like that and there is no point trying to redeem themselves, you've already decided they're useless.

If instead we said:

> *'I feel upset when you leave clothes on the floor and coffee cups on the table. Please clear up.'*

…we've done several things. We've told them our own feelings – not something they can deny. We've said exactly what it was they DID we'd like to have been different – a learning point for the future, and not a personal attack. And we've asked them to do something about it – a solution they can apply, and then no more hard feelings.

HOW TO USE AN 'I' STATEMENT

One vital technique to use when building communication is an 'I' statement. 'I' statements are all about being able to say what 'I want' and what 'I need'. They help the person speaking, and the person being spoken to, to be clear about what is really going on.

When you use an 'I' statement, you are:

▶ specific about what you want
▶ given the chance to recognize and say how you feel
▶ able to help other people understand what you want
▶ clear, honest and direct
▶ able to make your point without blaming, criticizing or judging other people.

'YOU' STATEMENTS

When we're upset we sometimes blame the other person for what has happened. 'Look what you made me do' or 'You make me so angry!' We can also use 'YOU' statements to deny responsibility for angry or critical remarks by implying they belong to someone else: 'Everyone thinks it's your fault.'

'You' statements seldom give the other person a chance to understand what we're upset about, how we feel or why, or give them an opportunity to make any changes. 'You' statements may be a way of not being overwhelmed by anger or despair. Instead of 'owning' feelings, we hold them at arm's length: 'One feels like that, doesn't one?' 'That's how you do it, don't you?' But instead of helping, they make the other person defensive and increase hostility and conflict.

WHAT AN 'I' STATEMENT DOES

Using an 'I' statement respects the other person and their point of view. It helps you say what you feel and want but avoids making the other person feel like the problem. This makes it far easier for both of you to come up with a solution – they can feel part of the solution, not all of the problem – and to take responsibility and act positively.

It can take some time to get into the habit of using 'I' statements. Most of us have had a lifetime of being told it's selfish or big-headed to say 'I'. But the more you use them, the more you'll find they work and help you and the other person feel good about the exchange.

An 'I' statement:

▶ describes the behaviour you are finding difficult
▶ explains the effect it has on you

- ▶ tells the other person how you feel about it
- ▶ invites them to join you in finding a solution.

For example:

> 'When I come home and find you haven't done your chores I feel really upset and angry. I feel as if you're taking me for granted and not listening to me. I'd like you to do the chores we've agreed, when we've agreed. If you're having a problem with that, let's talk about it.'

Using 'I' statements with teenagers can turn conflict into discussion as, above all, it respects the other person's point of view and their ability and willingness to negotiate and compromise.

Insight

The good news is that teenagers love their parents and want their attention and approval. They are far more likely to turn out to be like you than you think. The warning we need to heed therefore is that we need to be who we want to be in order for them to be what we would like them to be. Do as I say, not as I do...is probably the most futile statement to make to a child or young person!

What is behind conflict?

That seems to be a lot of different issues, and we could spend a whole book exploring them one by one (and I have – see the end of this chapter...). But the reality is that, most of the time, what we're arguing about is not actually the reason we're in conflict. Remember the Behaviour, Feelings, Needs Fountain. This is similar, in that a row over whether your teenager comes in on time and eats the food you make for them can actually be about your feelings of rejection and loss at their separation from you. Once upon a time, they wanted to share dinner times with you and ate the food you lovingly prepared. Now, their friends are more important to them than you and by turning up their nose at your meal, you feel as if they are throwing your love back in your face.

It doesn't matter what the problem or issue is, the strategies for getting it sorted are the same. Whether it's about sex, drugs and rock and roll, money, eating or body piercings, you need to employ the same techniques and strategies, some of which we've already discussed. You'll need to keep in mind Active and Reflective Listening, using 'I' statements and Open Questions. You'll want to treat your teenager with respect, to practise what you preach and to jump off that roundabout of circular arguments. You'll accept and acknowledge their feelings and look for the needs underlying their behaviour. Making the time, and making it easy, to have relaxed discussions with them can allow you to listen to their points of view and express your own.

PICK YOUR BATTLES

It's important to pick and choose the situations over which you want to disagree. You'll 'win' more often if the battle is about something you have good reason to want to insist upon. In other words, something which you might reasonably ask them to agree upon, or compromise over. The more fights you have over trivia or your personal taste as opposed to theirs – or their beliefs as opposed to yours – the more often you will get tied up in destructive and futile arguments. If you reserve 'no' for the few occasions when you feel strongly, your teenager is more likely to respect your point of view and come around with good grace.

When you and your teen aren't getting on, every little annoyance can blow up into a grand stand-up row. The trick is to save disputes for the important things – and to make those fights constructive discussions rather than conflicts. Try this exercise to work out your priorities. Sit down and write out:

- ▶ the things you really don't want happening
- ▶ the things that just get on your nerves
- ▶ the things you actually like about your teenager.

RED, YELLOW AND GREEN

You can see these three categories as the three colours of a traffic light:

- ▶ RED is the STOP sign: something you really need your teenager to change or not do.
- ▶ YELLOW is WARNING: something that puts you on edge that they should be aware of.
- ▶ GREEN is GO: something you really like and they might think about doing more, as a way of getting the balance right.

Complete the categories and talk over what you've written with your teenager. Why do these come to mind? Can you think about earlier times when these things have pleased or annoyed you? What does it remind you of when your teen does them? Sometimes what annoys or hurts us in the 'here and now' is more about an echo from the past than about what your teenager is actually doing. If you can locate the real source of your distress you may find the present behaviour worries you less.

Think of the relationships in a family as a piggy bank. Each time you have a row – and make an entry in the red or yellow category – you take a coin out. If you're forever taking out, pretty soon the bank is empty and you have nothing left. But every time you put a coin in – by making an entry in the green column – you fill up the bank. Having disputes does less harm to family harmony if you keep filling the bank as well as taking away.

> **Insight**
>
> If you want them to listen to you about the red issues, and have a discussion about the yellow ones, the best tactic is to find as many green ones as you can to praise them and thank them about, before asking to discuss the others.

PROBLEM SOLVING – A SIX-POINT PLAN

When you hit a point of disagreement or conflict, the first thing you need is calm. Call a time out and agree you'll work through a six-point plan.

1 Focus on what they need

Flexibility, defiance and structure: Young people need flexibility and to be allowed to rebel, but they also need rules, consistency and structure. The trick is to make these rules something that they agree to and understand. Say: 'These are the rules, take it or leave it', and they'll probably leave them. A system that runs on negatives – don't do this, no doing that, you shouldn't, mustn't, can't – is far less likely to be effective than one that has positive values as its basis. Focusing on pointing out what they did right, rather than what they did wrong, and asking them to do what you want rather than what you don't want, is far more likely to come up with the goods.

For you to affirm them: It's also important to be generally affirming about your adolescent. Don't only praise or thank them for specific actions, when they've done something. When anyone only gets 'a stroke' – a positive act or verbal affirmation – after particular events, their self-esteem becomes tied to activity; they get the idea that they must do something to please you and that your pleasure is dependent on their fulfilling tasks or actions. Instead of an overall sense of self-worth, they'll only feel good about themselves when getting praise and be dependent on other people's view of them, not on their own self-image. Teenagers need your time and attention, your good regard and praise – but praise for themselves, not yourself. Parents frequently bask in the congratulations and admiration of others for their child, as if nothing their child does or is, is by their own efforts – it's all down to their parents. You may be proud of your children and you may have good reason to feel you have a lot to do with their achievements, but let them take the credit for themselves. Being proud of them too often comes across as pride of ownership – as if it's you who should take the praise for whatever they've done, not them. Being proud for them puts the achievement squarely where it belongs – in their hands.

It's a good idea to cast your mind back to the way your parents treated you when you were a teenager. Did they thank you, make affirming statements about you, praise you? How did their interaction make you feel? Do you want to do the same – or something very different? The aim might be to be the parent we would like to be and wished we had had, and to that end, to become practised in giving strokes. A stroke a day keeps the doctor away…

Strokes

A 'stroke' is a way of giving value – any action that tells someone you're happy to see them, pleased to be with them and glad about something they might have done. Strokes may be verbal, when you say 'Thank you' or 'You did so-and-so – that was good'. They can also be actions such as making someone a cup of coffee or giving them a hug. When we give strokes it 'models' behaviour – lets people see how nice it is and how to do it. Give strokes and you soon find them coming back at you.

To own their own bodies: Let young people own their own bodies. It can be hard, as a parent, to see or accept the boundary that separates you and your child. After all, what seems to be just a few scant years ago, they were a twinkle in your eye and then a tiny speck of your own body. For nine months, they occupied their mother's body and it can be very difficult to let go of that sense of connection, of their being an extension and a part of you. This shows in what may seem, to the adult saying it, as joking or loving remarks and habits. 'Put a sweater on, I'm feeling cold!' may seem a harmless and affectionate bit of family banter, but what it also says is that you think you speak for them, answer for them and can act for them, for example: 'Paul wants to be an astronaut', 'Mum I haven't wanted to be an astronaut since I was five!', 'Don't contradict your mother, Paul!' or 'She takes sugar in her coffee', 'Dad, I'm not dumb and I've been having my coffee black without sugar for ages', 'Don't be cheeky!' None of these may matter individually but they add up and deny them their own feelings, thoughts and choices.

Privacy: Young people need privacy. Reading their diaries or listening in to phone calls, discussing them with their teachers or others behind their backs, only underlines that you don't trust or respect them or feel that they are capable of making decisions or choices. Encourage their autonomy and show respect if they're having a hard time. They are far more likely to come to you for help and support if you've given them the chance to try on their own than if you won't let go. This does not contradict the rule that computer and phone use is liable to your checks as and when you see fit. With cyber-bullying and the potential for misuse, both are special cases. But it should be something you do openly and after discussion, not behind their backs.

Communication: Of course, finding out what they need calls for all of your listening skills. Asking too many questions is often felt as intrusive and controlling. You can show an interest without it appearing to be an interrogation, using openers and reflective and active listening.

2 Consider your own feelings
Accept that anyone hates to be made redundant: By acknowledging your teenager's freedom, you are making yourself redundant. If you are going to succeed in letting go – by not fixing all their problems for them – you need to feel needed, wanted and essential in other parts of

your life. Parents often feel guilty about doing things for themselves; they feel that it deprives their children and makes them selfish and bad parents. In fact, the more you are able to take your own feelings and needs into account, the more you may be able to give your teen what they really need from you.

3 Ideas storm

We've already touched on ideas storming – a game or technique that really helps you solve problems and come up with solutions. It has the added bonus of giving participants a good laugh and drawing people together. Try this exercise for a quick demonstration of how it works. Get a sheet of paper, give yourself five minutes and write down as many uses as you can think of for a cork.

Done? Did you think of using it as pincushion, a doorstop, a toy for your cat or hamster, eye make-up if lightly charred? What about cutting it up into coins and use as gambling chips for a game of poker? Some of the ideas you might have come up with would be sensible and practical, some might work and some would be fanciful. The point about ideas storming is that sometimes, when we let our imaginations run riot, we find that the most unlikely solutions could work.

Explain the problem – for example, you need a way of stopping the arguments about doing homework over weekends. It is important to be clear about the problem. If you are vague, contradictory or are only seeing the difficulty from one point of view, you may find it harder to reach a resolution. Saying you want a way of enforcing homework done by Friday night, for example, is unlikely to get much co-operation from your teen. Since the real problem, most of the time, is the argument caused by your difference of opinion, focus on that. ANY solutions can then be put forward. In an ideas storming session, everyone is allowed their say and no idea is out of bounds.

Elect one member of your group to be the recorder and another to be timekeeper. The recorder lays out a large sheet of paper. Set yourself a time limit – 20 minutes is usually enough to get the creative juices going – but not so much that people run out of steam. At this stage, what is most important is that the solutions need not be sensible, workable or even desirable. Get every single person to jump in with as many ideas as they can, and write every single one of them down WITHOUT COMMENT: 'We can do it Sunday night', 'Stop worrying', 'Make them do it as soon as they come home on Friday', 'Pay someone on the internet to do it' – at this point every solution should be recorded, with no criticism or complaint.

The recorder should also function as a facilitator, pulling anyone up who pours cold water on anyone for their remarks, or tries to discuss them at this juncture. You'll find out why silly suggestions are welcome in ideas storming when you go on to the next stage. Once the time limit is up and you've put all your ideas down, take a break. Then, start at the top of your list and talk over each one. Don't dismiss anything out of hand, but do ask everyone what they think about it. Why not, in this instance, accept the 'Stop worrying' solution? Think about it and then explain why you'd find this hard or impossible. Explaining your point of view allows you to think it over – there is just an outside possibility they might be right – or gives you the chance to have them listen to how you feel. Paid cheats may be out of the question, but do they need some extra help at the moment? Leaving it to Sunday night may seem unacceptable, but if the issue is that they feel too tired to work on Friday night, have too much to do on Saturday, why is Sunday so hard for you to accept?

The key to ideas storming is that, hidden among all the jokes, dross and rubbish, you are likely to find a gem of a solution that you might otherwise not have discovered. Done properly, it also allows the whole family the chance to feel brought together in the search for a solution. Young people can be responsible, caring and sensible – if allowed to be so. The final benefit is that a solution that has been genuinely created and agreed upon by everyone becomes theirs. Most of us want to kick against rules that have been imposed upon us from above. When the solution is something we have had some input into knowing is necessary, we 'own' it. It's our rule and we have a vested interest in making it work.

IDEAS STORMING WORKS BECAUSE:

- ▶ Everyone has, and everyone knows they have, as much right to speak out as anyone else.
- ▶ Everyone has, and everyone knows they have, as much chance of having their solution taken seriously as anyone else.
- ▶ It's fun.

- ▶ It helps you think of difficulties as challenges that can be overcome, not problems that can't be solved.
- ▶ It casts young people as part of the solution rather than all of the problem.

4 Have a family round table discussion

Adults often use 'family discussions' as a way of telling their children what they have decided to do. It isn't, however, a true family round table unless you listen as much, if not more, than you talk and unless young people are given as much space and respect to have their say as adults. Round table talks may not always be what you need. There will be plenty of times when simply having the time and space to talk with and listen to someone else in the family is important. Try to make a point of allowing every member of the family some time to simply talk and be heard by you and by the other adults. But a family parliament is an ideal way, not just of keeping in touch, but also of pulling everyone together. It's above all a good technique to try if you are having problems and need to clear the air and one that, if used regularly, can head off disagreements. If you feel that your teenager is too young to give their views, or that you are uncomfortable about listening to them, this may be a difficult exercise for you to become accustomed to. It may seem false or awkward to think about sitting round a table actually explaining your views or listening to someone else's, but however silly all this sounds, the fact is that it can be enormously helpful.

The difference between a dictatorship and a democracy is the assembly. In the days when city states were small, all the members entitled to vote would come together to voice their opinions and vote. As populations became bigger, those with a vote would use it to put their choice of elected member into a senate or parliament, to discuss and legislate. You can run your family as a dictatorship, where only the adults have a say, or you can claim you're presiding over a democracy where your children are too young to be able to make choices. If you do, don't forget what usually happens in such systems. The oppressed peoples either overthrow the state in bloody revolution, or emigrate and never come back.

There are three main rules to make a family round table discussion work:

- ▶ Owning what you say
  The most important rule is that everyone has to 'own' what they say. That means, everything you put forward has to be your own

thoughts and feelings and you should acknowledge them as such, using 'I think' or 'I feel'. No one can say 'So-and-so says…' or 'Everyone knows…' or talk about what other people do or what you think they think. You can talk about how other people's behaviour affects you, by saying 'When you do such-and-such, I feel…', but the aim is to put your point of view, not to criticize or attack other people. The key is confronting problems, not people.

▶ Equality

Everyone, from oldest to youngest, is to have an equal turn to speak and to be heard. You might like to go round the table letting each person say one thing, to start. Then take turns to add to the discussion. You can use an object handed round to signify whose turn it is to speak and ask everyone to keep the rule about only talking when they have had it handed on to them. It helps to appoint one person to act as the 'facilitator' for a family round table, and to have each member of the group take it in turns to play this role. The facilitator ensures that everyone takes it in turns to speak and not interrupt.

▶ Consensus

The eventual aim of your discussion is to find a space where everyone feels they have been heard and appreciated, and have heard and appreciated everyone else's point of view. There should be no winners or losers, but an all-round agreement on the outcome. To that end, no one is to be shouted down for what they say. Discuss the points rather than arguing with the person. Set aside time for the discussion and allow everyone a chance to speak, as many times as they like.

5 Draw up a contract

Having ideas stormed and discussed, you need a clear way of keeping track of the agreed changes and how you're all going to make these changes. To do that, you should draw up a contract.

The idea is to write down exactly what everyone has said they will do. The key is that it shouldn't be one-sided, with one person or a few people asked to make an effort or making changes and other people acting as usual. Work out a fair exchange and one you can all agree.

Make a precise record, including:

▶ what you've all agreed to do
▶ how you agree to do it

- ▶ when you agree to do it by
- ▶ for how long you have agreed to do this.

Everyone should sign the contract, and have a copy for themselves. You could pin up the original somewhere you can all check it out, such as on the fridge in the kitchen.

6 Follow up
Review the contract and the agreed changes regularly. If the terms are not being met, discuss why and whether the contract needs to be redrawn or whether something needs to be adjusted.

There are several very good spin-offs to this form of discussion. One is that it means you no longer have to be – you no longer should be – in the position of policing your family. If two or more of your children have an argument, they should bring it to the round table discussion – but it's their responsibility, not yours, to sort it out. If one of the younger members of the family and an adult has a disagreement, it's up to the ones involved to settle it, not the role of one adult alone, or of older children to appoint themselves as proxy parents and tell off the younger ones. This puts a stop to one parent feeling they have to mediate between the other parent and children, when they should be having their own dialogue, or one parent being cast in the role of disciplinarian when the argument may be between the other parent and teen, or of older children bullying younger ones. Another benefit is that if agreed changes are not fulfilled, you have every right to insist.

GIVING IN TO FANTASY

Sometimes young people desperately want things they can't have. We may be sympathetic to young children wanting the moon, but somehow when it's a teenager the response is often to feel impatient that they can't be more reasonable. But why should they? Sometimes, dreams and ambitions need to be outrageous to give us a challenge. And often we can't help what we desire, even if it is clearly beyond our reach. Instead of laughing at them, or trying to be reasonable with them, one helpful response could be to Give In To Fantasy. This means saying what we, as a parent, would actually love to do: 'Darling, if I could, I would'. Try 'If I had a magic wand, if I could possibly make it so, I'd give you exactly what you want!' It sounds ridiculous, and it sounds like something you'd say to a five-year-old. Even 15- (or 55-) year-olds respond to the love and the intention behind the promise.

Jamie's son Mitch had been moping over a girl he had seen at a gig with his friends – she was three years older, at university and going out with his cousin. Jamie was seriously smitten but the girl was definitely out of his reach. His brother and sisters had laughed at him, while his mother had been sympathetic but tried to reason with him. Finally, after three weeks of misery, Jamie took Mitch out to a coffee bar on Saturday morning and said 'Mate, I wish I could do something for you. I wish I could make her notice you, do something amazing and change the world so she'd be free for you, swoop down and tell her what she's missing. If I could, I would!' Mitch was so touched at this father's sincerity that he laughed and they began to joke about what he could do if he really tried. From that moment, Mitch got his longings into perspective and under control.

HOW SHOULD YOU APPROACH THE ISSUE OF BEDTIMES WITH TEENAGERS?

If you thought struggles over bedtimes and sleep were only a feature of childhood, think again. Once your children move to secondary school and enter adolescence, it can start all over again. You may have had to cajole and use all sorts of skills to get your rules to stick with a child, but at least ultimately you had the greater authority – and size! – of an adult over a small person. Once they are teens, you may lose some of that authority, and are more than likely to be eye to eye or even looking up at them. So using all your skills of discussion, negotiation and debate are what you will fall back on.

Talk through your concerns and ask for theirs, and ask that you arrive at a workable solution. Help kids understand that this is not you being a spoilsport but a genuine issue over the fact they need more sleep because of changes in their bodies.

▶ Point out that for their health, wellbeing and future success, 9¼ hours of sleep a night is essential. That's not you being a spoilsport, it's a medical fact. They can't get by on 5 hours on weekdays and expect to catch up by sleeping all day over the weekends – it doesn't work like that. So the only issue is how you'll all make it easy to get in the hours.

- Make a stand on bedtimes, even if they are big, grown up teenagers. Insist on no caffeine drinks after lunch (some so-called energy fizzy drinks targeted at teenagers contain more caffeine than a pot of coffee), healthy eating and exercise as a part of this.
- Make it a rule, and enforce the rule, that there is no electronic media in bedrooms. Hard as it may seem, you may have to accept keeping to the rule yourselves to be able to insist on this. No TV, no games consoles, no mobile phones or tablets or laptops or notebooks or even music players with ear buds or headphones. Allow music players as long as played out loud but at night enforce quiet, calm music only.
- Set a bedtime and keep that bedtime the same on the weekends as it is on weekdays. This is because when you start playing around with and disrupting a pattern it's that much harder to adjust the internal clock from one time to another. If you must, allow a one hour later wake and bedtime on Saturday and Sunday – but no more than one hour. The reality is it's far easier to leave it as it is.
- Ask your teens to let friends know that you operate a curfew not only on being home by bedtime but also on accepting incoming contact, whether calls, texts or online chat after the beginning of the bedtime routine. Calls and other contact must end then. If their friends have different rules explain that's up to their parents – in your house your care for them means this is the way you do it. Full stop.
- Agree and keep to a bedtime routine. The fact is that if you simply go from toddler to childhood to teenage bedtime routines, only changing some of the details but assuming that everyone has a routine and that's that, it will be so much easier.
- As part of the routine, give your teen cues that it is time to go to sleep. Switch off TVs and other media – you can record or time shift to catch up on programmes you want to watch when they are in bed, or next day earlier in the evening. Dim the lights and be available to them, to say goodnight and have those all important chats. Reverse this when it's time to get up – flood their rooms with light, either natural or artificial.
- As well as offering reviving snacks and drinks when your teens come home from school or being out in the day, suggest they might like half an hour of quiet time for a siesta or just a rest afterwards. Even ten minutes of 'shut eye' can help, and

half an hour's sleep (use an alarm clock to make it no more than that) can be added to the 9¼ daily total, which can mean a half an hour later bedtime.

▶ Avoid conflict before they go to bed. If there is a row brewing, state what the disagreements are and ask that you set them aside until the next day when you can discuss it when both are calm.

HELPING THEM PICK THEIR BATTLES

There are things we can change, and things we can't. I'd like to be a foot taller, 5 kilos lighter and fit into some jeans I've had for 20 years. There is nothing I can do about the height – even stilettos aren't going to make me that much taller. So worrying, obsessing, moaning about being a little short-arse is going to get me precisely nowhere. Except make me miserable, and upset and bore everyone around me. But I can do something about the weight, and the jeans, through healthy eating and exercise. And when I'm feeling better about my shape and size, my height becomes not only immaterial, but something that in fact I'm fine about.

Every aspect of your life that you would like to be different can be subjected to the same test – can I do something about it and if so what? If I can't, does it help to complain? Or might I be able to change my attitudes towards the problem, if I can't change the thing itself?

Teenagers often bemoan aspects of themselves and their lives. So this is a really important lesson to pass on to them. It's often tempting when they complain about their appearance, their friends, their schoolwork, or their parents, to cut them short, be impatient or give them a lecture. Instead, sit down, sympathize, and say you'd love to help, so why don't you work out:

▶ What they'd like to be different
▶ If it could be altered
▶ If so, how and what could they do, and you support them in doing
▶ If not, what they might do now, in that light

Once you've been through this exercise a few times, you'll find it easier to get them to approach all problems in the same way – what, if, how and what now. Make sure you're applying it to your own problems, to model the strategy!

KNOWING WHOSE RESPONSIBILITY THIS IS

One of the skills you'll need as the parent of a teenager is to know what is yours to manage and what is theirs, to separate their problems from your own. Just as teenagers are struggling to set their own boundaries, establish their own independence and separate from their parents, so parents in a way have to do the same. You need to help them, and help yourself, by knowing where you and your sphere of influence ends – and theirs begins.

As a parent you often have a tendency to want to sort out your teenager's problems. After all, when they were babies it's what you had to do – recognize when they were hungry, cold, tired, or needing a cuddle – and satisfy that need. As a child, you did the same – protect them, nurture them, and care for them. Now they are a teenager, you may try to do as you have always done because you think that is the best thing you can do – protect, nurture and fix anything that hurts or worries them. It may seem the best thing to do, but it is not always the most helpful thing to do.

Sometimes parents can't separate their own needs from their teenager's. In seeking to do your best you may stray into making inappropriate demands to try and satisfy the wrong need. When you are feeling protective about something that is upsetting them, or frustrated or angry about something your teenager is or isn't doing, it usually helps to get clear in your own mind why it is a problem for you.

Your problem or theirs?
Consider these scenarios:

▶ April is furious because two of her friends are excluding her.
▶ Jan is miserable because a boy she likes is paying more attention to her friend.
▶ Will wants you to buy him a new phone because he's broken the one he's had for six months.

Whose problems are these? It can be painful to hear that your teenager is feeling sad – feeling left out, losing out with a boy or girlfriend, having something they value go wrong. It can remind you of times in your own life when something similar happened. You may be keen to fix the situation they are suffering now: 'Because I know what it's like and I don't want you to suffer as I did.'

That's exactly the time to draw a clear boundary and decide whether it's your problem or theirs. It may feel hard but it's often important to resist getting sucked in. You don't help your child if you take it personally. That often comes from a secret and forlorn hope that you can rewrite the past. If you can help them, you almost feel it might mean you wouldn't have experienced that same loss in your own past. Your desire to 'fix' the problem can be a way of easing your own pain – past or present. You need to be able to manage your own feelings in order to respond helpfully to your child – to bite a lip and stand back and let them manage their own discomfort. You can let them know you care by listening and being there, which can't necessarily take the pain away, but can help them cope and find their own resources.

In all these scenarios, it is the teenager who has the problem. Your problem might be in wanting to do something – anything! – about it. But the best strategy would be to AIM to help. AIM stands for Acknowledge, Identify and Move on. It's a very useful strategy for dealing with many issues. So, you:

▶ Acknowledge feelings: 'You sound sad/angry/fed up.'
▶ Identify needs: 'You wanted him to like you/it was something you'd wanted for a long time.'
▶ Move on: 'What would you like to say to him/do now?'

Whose problems are these?
You may be annoyed about something your teenager has done but if you want the situation to change you need to identify where the responsibility really lies. If you're the one who amends your behaviour because of something they do and then get upset, maybe the solution is to stop compensating. If you're late because they are late, analyse the situation, and lay out the new rules: 'Tomorrow I leave on time, whatever state you're in. If you're not ready you'll just have to make your own way to school. What could you do to make sure that doesn't happen? Is there anything I can do to help?' You might agree to give them a five-minute warning, and help them prepare their school bags the night before. You might need to acknowledge that it is your problem: 'Pete, I get upset when towels are left on the floor, not on the rail. I'd like you to hang up your towel in future please so I don't get angry.' Or 'I get worried when you don't get home at the time you said. If it happens again I'd like you to ring and tell me you're running late please. If you've got a

problem with getting home, tell me and let's see if we can sort it.' But if it's your problem, deal with it. If it's theirs encourage and support them to deal with it.

Ideas to get the conversation going

Talking with our teenagers can be a joy. They're at such an interesting stage of their lives – struggling with the big questions, alert and aware before becoming cynical. Encouraging them to communicate with us not only keeps the family ties strong, it opens our eyes too. And the more we can 'just chat' the more likely it is they will come to us when they have something important to say or ask. So how can we make sure we keep talking? There's a trick to this. You need to avoid questions that actually have the effect of stopping the conversation dead. 'Closed' questions do this, and are where you ask something that can be answered 'Yes', 'No', 'Meh' or even 'Duh!' If you ask 'Did you have a good day in school today' it really does only call for one of those. Directional questions can also block off the flow – 'What did you do in school today' may elicit 'History, maths and science…' and not much else since you were clearly focused on what went on in class and little else. In a directional question you decide the area of enquiry, and that may not be something the person you're wanting to open up wants, or has a lot, to talk about. When you use a closed or directional question the other person can also feel that it's an inquisition that's on offer, not a conversation. Inquisitions are where parents busybody into their children's lives, trying to catch them out, control them and make them feel bad. Conversations are two-way, where both or all parties give and take. Everyone contributes and learns from a conversation, and is on the same level. Conversations are about caring and sharing, listening and being heard. Conversations are what help bring families together.

OPEN QUESTIONS

So how can you start and continue conversations? You need to use Open Questions. An open question is when the answer has to be more than one or two words. Open questions are not just about facts but about feelings and opinions. Open questions say 'I'm interested in what you think and feel and I'm listening to you.' An open question rather than 'Did you have a good day in school today' or 'What did you do in school today', might be 'Tell me about your day today'. Tell me about your day allows the other person to choose which bit they feel was important to them. It might not be about what they learnt in class but about something that caught their attention and interest on the way to or from school. It might be about something worrying or unpleasant in school, or outside. It might be about something triumphal or joyous around their friendships. Encouraged to reflect and enlarge, and given free direction, you're likely to get a whole lot more back than from a closed or directed question. Your aim is twofold: to learn about your child, and to allow your child to be able to express and accept their own feelings and opinions. Being given a forum for expressing their activities, feelings and opinions gives young people a sense of entitlement, of self-esteem and self-confidence.

What they will need is your trust. Children will soon learn not to confide in you if you use their confidences back at them. If they tell you something that worries or alarms you of course you need to talk this over with them. What you don't do is fling it back in their face during an argument, allow it to be used in sibling arguments or take it outside the family without their express consent.

GIVE OF YOURSELF

Another aspect it's useful to consider is your own example. From the time they can talk children are fascinated by their parent's life, past and present. They really do want to know about what you did as a child, or do now. Of course, it's all in the way you tell it. If all they ever hear is you drawing comparisons and criticizing them and their world, you are likely to get a bored 'Oh Mum, not again!'. But if your stories are just that – stories about your life and your feelings and opinions, with space for them to contrast and compare – what you will be doing is modelling how to communicate, how to share.

So keep in mind these rules:

- ▶ Use open questions
- ▶ Listen and hear
- ▶ Keep their trust
- ▶ Share something of yourself

We've talked about giving strokes – those verbal or non-verbal affirmations that show you value someone. Make a list of all the strokes you like to receive, and want to give. You might think of:

▶ Hugging someone.
▶ Patting them on the arm.
▶ Saying 'Thank you'.
▶ Saying 'I really like it when you…'
▶ Making them a cup of tea.
▶ Having their favourite biscuit or cake in the tin.
▶ Pointing out a programme or film that's on and you know they'd enjoy.
▶ Clipping an article out of the paper or magazine that you know would interest them.
▶ Doing a chore you know they dislike.
▶ Saying 'Oh, it's nice to see you – I was thinking about you today.'
▶ Fill in your own – those you'd like to receive and those you'd like to give. Now:

Make a point of giving at least one from the list today, and every day. And show your list to your family so they know what you'd love to receive.

KEY POINTS

1 Teenage years can be the hardest time for parents. It is the teenager's job to prepare themselves to leave you, and it is your job to help them do so.

2 Teenagers want, and need, control over their lives. They have to achieve this while their bodies and emotions are changing and their parents might be having a mid-life crisis of their own. With 15 years meeting 40 years, there are bound to be clashes.

3 They still need you to value them and want your approval. You can help by maintaining the family's structure and togetherness. Two ways to help are to ensure that there are regular family meals and that electronics are banned in bedrooms or other isolated areas.

4 With incompatible jobs to do, you and your teenager are bound to have arguments. The answer is to use strategies, like those in the chapter. Listen, ask yourself what is underneath the behaviour – and sometimes, just put your foot down!

5 A teenager's bad behaviour is usually a way of trying to show, or 'act out,' bad feelings. Understanding the needs that may lie beneath the behaviour is the key tool in resolving most clashes.

6 Good communication between teens and adults is a necessity. One of the best ways to get there is to practise, and then use, the 'I' statement – and then lose the unhelpful 'You' statement that can come so easily to a stressed parent's lips.

7 Pick your battles and prioritize. You will 'win' your arguments more often if you pick and choose the situations over which to disagree – the areas in which you have good reasons to want to insist. Also, explain this concept to them so that they can use it in their own life.

8 Have regular Family Round Table meetings. You can then use these to draw up a contract with your teen when you have discussed and agreed what everyone will, and will not, do.

9　There is an understandable instinct to 'do everything for them.' But, remember the main job of their teenage years is to respect their struggle and let them find their own solutions as much as possible.

10　The teenage years can be problematic ones, but they can also be the happiest. The biggest reward for good teenage parenting is that your young one will fly the nest well equipped for life outside and then will always willingly return to visit you many times in the years to come.

Teenagers in a chapter? I've written a whole book on the subject so if you'd like more, do look at *Raise A Happy Teenager* (Teach Yourself).

BEING HAPPY

How are you doing with the fun sheet? Here are a few more ideas to add – do your own!

Small things	Medium things	Big things
Play music. Sit in the sun and do nothing. Take a nap. Sit and talk with your teenagers.	Make pancakes with your teenagers and see how many different fillings you can come up with.	Go to a concert. Throw a barbecue with your friends and your teenagers' friends. Go to a theme park. Take a trip on a narrowboat.

6

....

Empty nest and boomerang kids

In this chapter you will learn:
- *About Empty Nest Syndrome and why it is so hard to let children go*
- *About the three basic roles we play – Child, Adult and Parent*
- *To make an Exit Plan to help your children leave home*

Once the home begins to empty with children departing, all remaining members of the family will find themselves going through a period of adjustment and renegotiation. Those left at home can feel bereft. Parents can feel redundant, rejected, passed by. It's a time of life when parents can feel decidedly unhappy, and pessimistic about getting back the joy they might have once taken in their family and their lives.

Family life is all about change, and never more so than when your children begin to leave home. Some parents look towards it with dread while some see it as a cause for celebration. Without a doubt, most families have to go through a stressful period, whether this is the first child to leave and you still have one or more at home, or whether it's the last and that means you are left alone. And it's also often true that even if you had looked forward to this moment and saw it in a positive light, the process of change itself can take the shine off it. Change can be as hard and as stressful to manage if you see it as a positive event as it can when you expect it to be one to fear.

Empty Nest Syndrome

Why is it so hard – why do we talk in terms of an Empty Nest Syndrome? Surely the time your children leave home is exciting and enjoyable and the cause of much happiness to you all? You get your home and life back, to do with as you wish. And they journey off into the sunrise, to pursue their dreams and ambitions and do as they please, as they've probably been demanding the chance to do for the last few years.

However, it's often not quite as easy as that. Having and bringing up children is an overwhelmingly all embracing experience. From babyhood to adolescence, your children demand your attention and fill your lives. Every room in the house contains their belongings, every moment of your life revolves around their care and every decision you make has to be made with them in mind; your life in effect is taken up by them and their needs. And this is true, even with teenagers when you have moments when the home is yours alone because they're off spending much of their time with their friends. Being immersed in your role as a parent means that when it seems to come to an end, as they leave home, you can feel bereft. It's as if you have been made redundant – the emotions are often overpoweringly of being rejected and passed over. Even if this is the first child to leave and you still have kids at home you may feel an era has ended and your job is at risk. And indeed, the children left behind can also feel as if they are in mourning, too. They lose a sibling and they also lose so much that was familiar. They might have been the youngest, the middle child or one of two. All of a sudden their position in the family alters and they can feel quite off balance. They have to adjust to being a new person themselves, as well as missing the companionship of another child – and that is true even if they had been at loggerheads much of the time.

WHEN THE LAST ONE GOES

But if this is your last or only child leaving, the effects can be devastating. The house is quiet, you are no longer on call, you are no longer responsible. For many parents, the years between a child arriving and that child leaving home are primarily focused on the progress and wellbeing of the child. You can get so caught up in bringing up your children that the contact you have between yourselves actually flows through them – it's about them, over them, around them. For the years leading up to this moment, your one to one adult relationship may have taken a back seat. With them gone, you may wake up to discover that your children were a vital link – the element binding you together and the conduit through which you carried on your relationship. Empty Nesters find themselves with a dilemma – will they rebuild the link, or find it has been severed?

How do you manage when children leave home? To get your happy back, you might have to make strenuous efforts to move on and process the change it brings, and accept that it can take some time.

6 tips for Empty Nesters or when children leave home

1 Practise
2 Accept change
3 Be open
4 Mourn
5 Celebrate
6 Take action

Practise. It really helps if, during the last few years your teenage children lived with you, you encouraged and supported them to have time away from you. This means letting them go on school trips, both overnight and for some days, and making it a priority to put aside money so you can afford that. It might also mean encouraging them to earn money so they can take holidays with friends, apart from you. It can come as a shock all round if their leaving home for college or a job is the first time they've spent a night away from you.

Accept change. It is a significant time in your life as well as theirs. Both parents, but fathers particularly, might seek to trivialize the experience, insisting it's not serious, it's not that bad, it's all a natural part of life so why make a fuss? The reality is that it's serious, it can be felt as being truly awful and while being a natural part of life that's no reason for it not to hurt. Acknowledge to each other, and to those around you, that this is hard – that's the first step in managing it.

Be open. Once you are being upfront about how it feels, you can share your emotions, and your struggle, with other parents in the same situation. You can take comfort in knowing you're not alone and swap tips on how to manage.

Mourn. If you want to move on to enjoying the benefits of your children leaving, you first need to go through the stage of recognizing and acknowledging the drawbacks. If you never mourn out loud, you get stuck in suppressed, hidden mourning, where you feel miserable but can't process it. Sniffle, weep, wail out loud and talk over all the things you're going to miss with them gone. Get a piece of paper and go to town, writing down everything that you can see as a minus with them being gone – such as their company, their liveliness, their conversation and the fact that they make you feel relevant, loved and wanted.

Celebrate. Once you've mourned, start looking on the bright side. For everything you've grieved as a loss, write down a plus. Such as, the cake you made or biscuits you bought to share with friends or your partner are still on the shelf an hour after you put them there, not plundered and half missing. And you can do things yourself spontaneously without having to plan for the other people in the house too. You can achieve or experience things you've always wanted to, but have never had the time or money to do.

Take action. Sometimes you need to push yourself to get out and take advantage of the bright side to your new situation. Look at your list of advantages and use it to compile an action plan, prioritizing the changes you'd like to make. Use your list of losses and drawbacks to help you think about the issues that might hold you back, and deal with them. Children leaving home can be the impetus we need to take up new opportunities in work and employment, new directions in personal development, and new chances in following dreams and ambitions.

REASSESS YOUR RELATIONSHIP

If you and your partner are still together, put that relationship under the spotlight now. Do you still love each other? Do you still do things together? Do you share emotions, thoughts and time? Parents in the throes of bringing up a family often put their own relationship on the back burner. Now's the time to bring it back to the fore. Remember what you had to begin with and consider what you have now. If you simply drift on after your children leave the chances are you might continue as if they were still there, needing your first attention. Instead, make each other your focus now and discuss what you should and could do to take advantage of this. If, as sadly happens too often, you feel that with your children gone you've woken up to find all you once had has gone and you're not sure what could replace it, consider asking for help and support and take the opportunity for relationship support or therapy. Many couples go through this crisis and then find that they can build on what they once had and the immense emotional investment they have made over the years, to come out with an even stronger, better, happier relationship. But it can sometimes help to get some professional support to make that jump and shake off the apathy that could have crept in over the years.

FINDING A NEW PARTNER

If you are on your own, then now is the time to see all the advantages of being unencumbered, and deciding what you want to do about it.

Most of us find our partners:

▶ through school or college
▶ at work
▶ through friends or family
▶ by meeting them at social events
▶ by getting to know them in our neighbourhood.

If you're going back to the dating scene after children have left home you may feel you have no access to a pool of ready, willing and available people yet when you think about this list, you still have most of the categories open to you – even college, if you take the opportunity to do some new training. And a few new categories may have opened up too, with new technology and new attitudes. You can also add:

▶ social networking on the internet
▶ dating agencies.

HOW TO WIDEN YOUR SOCIAL NETWORK

It may seem a terrible cliché, but now really is the time to join clubs and classes, to widen your social network as much as possible. Learn how to ballroom dance, do house maintenance, be a chef, or do creative writing. If you can make some time in your schedule, do some voluntary work locally. Go to places where you'll meet people, or help people and use it to get back your self-esteem and to make friends.

CHILDREN STILL AT HOME

If you do still have children at home, talk through with them how they might be feeling. They too might be struggling with feelings of loss but hampered by an anxiety that they're being unfair or silly, and so be reticent about discussing it. And if the sibling relationship had been fraught, they might be partly delighted to see the back of a brother or sister and glad to have more of the limelight now. That in itself may make them feel guilty, or confused if they then also find they are missing them. Helping them recognize a mix of emotions is normal and natural, and supporting them in expressing them, can be a great help. All of you may want to discuss how you keep in contact and what you do when the child who has left returns, for day or weekend visits or longer.

CONTACT WITH THE CHILD WHO HAS LEFT

To manage continuing contact you need to think about how the child who has left may feel, and be handling their lives. That in itself has some bearing on how we cope in their absence as well as when they return. While we are mourning and rearranging ourselves, the child who has left is off on a brand new adventure. Everything is new so there might be less of a struggle to adapt since getting used to something different is only to be expected. They may indeed be nervous and anxious and worried about their ability to cope, but by doing so in the company of other people in the same situation and with the support of those expecting them to need encouragement and help. They may be oblivious to how their parents feel.

How you articulate your feelings and make room for them to state theirs can set the tone for their success in having left home, and in your future relationship. Dumping your grief and loss on them can make them feel guilty. Just at the time when they need to be able to spread their wings and fly, unencumbered, the last thing they need is to be hindered by the idea that they are causing you pain. Whether you say so or not, young people can get the impression that not only is it their fault but that the correct remedy is for them to come home, or at least remain ultimately reliant on you, to give your life some meaning.

SETTING LIMITS ON CONTACT

Contact may be important for both of you, but it may be more useful for all of you to impose some limits on this. Daily texts or calls might feel reassuring and loving, and can be so. But, depending on the context and the content, can be preventing both sides from moving into this new era. Young adults who give up college or a job away from home to move back may do so because they have not felt supported and encouraged to manage their new demands. Regular contact can help them do so. But equally, some who retreat do so because the contact they have had has made them feel still children, still in need of being cared for and not able to stand on their own two feet.

Letting go of the parent role

And you do need to all be able to move into the next, new phase of parent/child relationships. When they do come back, whether it is for a short stay or longer, the balance between you should have altered. It's very easy, when your children return after an absence whether it is to go to college or begin working, to fall back on treating them exactly the same as you did when they were at home. And if you do this, the chances are that they will find themselves behaving in much the same way as they did too. The reason this happens is because we tend to fall into one of three fundamental roles in life when interacting with other people. If you think about it you'll recognize that you are a different person depending on who you are with, whether it's a workmate, a friend, your own parent, your partner or your child. With a colleague and a partner you are likely to be acting as an adult. With your own child, a parent. With your mother or father you might find yourself feeling, and behaving, like a child. Child, adult and parent are the three basic and important roles we play in life. It's clear you would in a lifetime progress from being a child to an adult and then a parent. But what might be less obvious is that we still function as all three, at many times in our lives.

FALLING INTO ROLES

People tend to fall into the role that corresponds with the role the other person they're with is playing. So, if you continue to be all parental to your children when they come home, they will continue to act as children. This can have serious and sad results. Conflict may continue, between you and them, and between siblings. Many family gatherings are ruined by adult children arguing bitterly, oblivious to the fact that they are in fact re-enacting childish arguments and disputes, often to the total confusion of their partners, and their own children. They don't feel able, and you may not allow them, to take responsibility for their own relationships – instead, you continue to monitor, comment and referee.

Responsibility for avoiding this rests with parents, and it's one of the tasks we have at the time they are old enough to leave home, to 'renegotiate the contract'. Whether we have been explicit about it or not, you and your children have a contract. If you have Family Round Table meetings, and discuss issues such as behaviour, rules, and chores in your family, you have made the contract explicit. You all know that mum and dad earn the money to pay the expenses, and do much to run the home. In exchange, children agree to take on certain responsibilities and to behave in certain ways.

RENEGOTIATING THE CONTRACT

You need to renegotiate the contract, and this may need all of you to sit down and ideas storm. What can you do?

1 Change your perception
   These are no longer your little children and you need to recognize and acknowledge the development that has happened.
2 Recognize the effect of child/adult/parent roles
   If we feel that our grown up children still expect to be looked after as if they were children, it's worthwhile looking at how we are acting towards them, and considering the influence this has. It's very easy for us to slip, lovingly, back into being cosseting, caring parents. The downside of that is it becomes equally easy for them to give up responsibility and fall back into being dependent. And with dependency often comes teenage behaviour – sulks, moods and demands. The only way to sidestep this is to jump tracks and get out of the parent/child relationship, into a more adult/adult one. Of course you are always their parents. But the parent of an adult child can expect a more mature and less tempestuous relationship than you might have come to accept with a teenager!
3 Discuss new rules and new boundaries
   You may all need to be quite open and unambiguous about what you would like from each other, and what you would expect to offer each other, to make this work. Sit down in a Family Round Table and ideas storm all the aspects of living together that you can see, or have already seen, might need to change. Agree all the pressure points and suggest ways round them.

They may want to come and go as they please; you will agree but ask in return they let you know if they are coming home for a meal, will be home late or are staying out. That's not checking up on them, it's simple courtesy, and the same as when you tell your partner if you have a late meeting or a date with friends. They might want to take advantage of the meal service, the laundry service, the ironing and cleaning service in the home. That's fine – but in return they do their share too, and pay towards the expenses. They will want to be treated with respect. Of course! But that means they must return the respect, and act as adults too.

Boomerang Kids

More and more adult children are returning home, as the so-called Boomerang Kids – young adults who move back in, having left home for a short time. It may be for a short period in between ending college and establishing their own household. That period may lengthen, either because they cannot find a home, or do not have the finances to afford one. Or it may be because home comforts and your attitude make it easier to remain, or harder to leave. Or, they may return after a crisis at college, at work or in a relationship, and again, get stuck and become for whatever reason reluctant to strike out again on their own.

There can be four reasons why young adults find it hard to leave home.

Unrealistic expectations
One may be that our expectations are unrealistic. In many families, it is assumed that once college is over or a job has been found that means the little birds are ready to fly the nest and make their own homes. But is this true? At 18 or 19, or even 21 or 22 and older, young people are still apprentice adults. It's hard enough having to adjust to all the demands the world makes on you outside the safe and straightforward world of school and college, without also having to negotiate the tricky rapids of managing your own home. It's not unreasonable to expect going out into the big wide world should be done in stages. First, adjust to college and having to oversee your own learning and make decisions about how you use it. Then, adjust to job seeking, job finding and hopefully job learning, where your

young person finds the environment in which they will grow to be self-sufficient. And only then, perhaps, are they ready to take on the far greater step of looking after themselves and running an establishment of their own, with all the responsibilities and work that entails.

Your needs hold them back

A second reason may be that you are holding them back. There may be conflict, you may be moaning and complaining about their being there, but the reality may be that your actions frustrate their leaving. If you are featherbedding them, making it just too easy to stay by doing everything for them and asking for no or very little money, they can hardly be forgiven for finding it far better to remain in the cosy parental home than risk the cold outdoors. And the reason you do it could be that having them there suits you just fine. Maybe having your child still dependent on you fulfils your needs, to feel wanted and useful. Having them go, after all, can feel as if you're redundant and on the shelf. If you don't have another way of feeling validated, keeping your children close by you can do the trick. You may also hate to see them go because they're company. A house full of children that suddenly empties can seem cold, quiet and lifeless and if much of your social life had revolved around being a parent, you may feel suddenly bereft and short of ideas on how to fill it. And yet another reason may be that children constitute an effective barrier between partners. If you have been used to carrying on your relationship through them and about them, once they are gone it can feel as if the ties that bound you have been severed and you are exposed. Instead of talking about them or to them, you have to face each other and talk about other things. After 18+ years of being parents, you may find that hard. And of course if you and your partner are no longer together, losing your children really does make you finally alone.

Their anxieties hold them back

The third reason may be that they feel scared of testing the waters, and far more inclined to stay where they are comfortable. This may be more than creature comforts that holds them at the parental home but also a crisis in confidence, where young adults simply do not feel resilient enough or competent enough to manage on their own. And it may go hand in hand with parents being reluctant to let go – if that's how you feel you may not have prepared them or given them sufficient confidence in their own abilities to cope, in order to have them remain close.

They can't afford it

The final reason can be that they can't find somewhere to live. This may be because there is a dearth of affordable housing for first timers in the area. They may not have found a job, or a job that pays sufficiently, to afford to be on their own.

THE EXIT PLAN

So how can you help them? What may be needed is an Exit Plan, that in fact you should be considering and putting in place from your child's last year in school, if not, in some aspects, even before that.

An Exit Plan is a way of addressing the issues that could come up when you and they approach their leaving home. It's a long term plan and you can chart the things you can and should do while they are still teenagers at home, and what comes into play when they leave to go to college or take up work.

Strengths, Weaknesses, Opportunities and Threats

What might help all of you would be to do a SWOT analysis.

SWOT stand for Strengths, Weaknesses, Opportunities and Threats.

Strengths are what you and your young person do well. We all have strengths, even if we don't realize what they might be. The trick is to recognize them, accept and develop them and use them, to our best advantage.

Weaknesses are what you and your young person do less well – the skills they may lack, or the attitudes that hold them back. The trick is to recognize and accept them as well, and to see how we can work around them so they don't pull us down.

Your Opportunities. These are all the other people, ideas, and situations around you that can help you achieve your goal.

Your Threats. While your weaknesses are the issues inside you that might hold you back, Threats are the things outside that could sabotage you.

	These help you get what you want	*These stop you getting what you want*
Inside you	STRENGTHS	WEAKNESSES
Outside you	OPPORTUNITIES	THREATS

When you look at your goal, which is to help your young adult leave home in the best possible way, what can help is to look at the things that can help you, both inside and out – your strengths and opportunities – and emphasizing them. It means looking at the things that can hinder you all, both inside and out – your weaknesses and threats – and working to tackle them.

This exercise can help you work out what you might need to do. In the chart, I've filled in some strengths and opportunities, weaknesses and threats, with this particular goal in mind: to help one young person leave home.

	These help you get what you want	These stop you getting what you want
Inside you	STRENGTHS Jack can cook for himself. He can budget. He wants to leave home soon. We would like the home to ourselves.	WEAKNESSES He can avoid doing things he doesn't like. He can be tempted to spend too much on going out with friends. I'll miss him.
Outside you	OPPORTUNITIES A friend also wants to leave home and is willing to flat share. He has a job.	THREATS His job doesn't pay very well. Flats are expensive around here.

USING EACH STRENGTH
How could you use and get the most out of each Strength? In this case, you can build on the positive feeling that Jack has about setting up in his own place. He has some skills in looking after himself – you could help him build more. And the fact that you can see advantages to his going means you have an incentive to help, support and encourage him to move it along.

IMPROVING EACH WEAKNESS
How could you improve each Weakness? You can stop condoning his avoidance of the chores he doesn't like doing, to help him get used to managing on his own. You can enforce some practical financial

decisions to let him learn how to pay essential bills before he spends on enjoying himself. And you can address the fact that his moving out will be a loss for you – the more you can manage it, the better he will too.

BENEFITTING FROM EACH OPPORTUNITY

How could you exploit and benefit from each Opportunity? In this case, you can support and encourage the two friends to think about flat share agreements to make living together easy, so their relationship can weather it and not break down – simple issues such as agreeing chores and responsibilities between them. You can be enthusiastic about his job and help him think in terms of doing well, looking to develop and expand his abilities, to stay there and indeed look for promotion.

LESSENING EACH THREAT

How could you lessen each Threat? Being supportive about his job can help him aim to see his salary increase in the future, and you might help him look at the possibilities of balancing a longer commute – or being further away from you – with cheaper housing in another neighbourhood, or in looking at bigger accommodation with extra flatmates to drive down the cost per head. Or indeed, supplementing his income with a weekend or evening job.

Now create your own SWOT chart. Thinking about your child leaving home – what are the Strengths and Opportunities, Weaknesses and Threats?

	These help you get what you want	These stop you getting what you want
Inside you	STRENGTHS	WEAKNESSES
Outside you	OPPORTUNITIES	THREATS

SO WHAT DO YOU NEED TO DO TO HELP THEM?

Create an Exit Plan, using the SWOT analysis to pinpoint what might help or hinder you. Draw up a schedule, with the end point being moving out, and suggest a timetable – will that be in a matter of a few months, six months or a year? Once you have an end point you can start adding in all the skills they need to learn in the interim, and all the issues you may need to tackle to get them there.

First, tackle the four reasons for staying – family assumptions, finding and affording a place to go, and your reservations and theirs.

Family assumptions

This may need a Family Round Table to thrash it out, as sometimes we do fall into unhelpful and outmoded attitudes, because that's the way it's always been. So we may be holding our children back from testing themselves, simply because that's the way our parents managed it. But equally, we may be expecting them to go without taking account of the present situation, which clearly does not make it easy for young people to manage on their own.

Finding and affording a place to go

Depending on where you live, it might have become difficult for young people to find affordable rented accommodation, or start on buying their own – or downright impossible. But the reality can be that young people shy away from accepting somewhere because it doesn't come up to the standards they've been used to, living with you. Sometimes they may need more than a nudge to accept that it won't be as comfortable or spacious or as well decorated as their parents home, because you've damn well spent 20+ years slaving away to afford that!

Helping them with affording it means primarily helping them learn to manage their cash. If they haven't already had an introduction into the mysteries of bank accounts, credit cards and other credit such as store cards, now is the time. For a current account it's always a good idea to open one in person at a bank – help them look for one that offers the best deal in interest or added value that applies to them. And make a point of discussing what happens and how much it costs if you go overdrawn, and how much credit costs if you max out your credit or store card and don't pay it all back.

FOUR TYPES OF MONEY

It can help to discuss and be firm about the idea that any money they have coming in – pay cheques, family gifts, extra earnings – should be divided into four sections.

▶ One is money you earmark each month, or week, for essential expenses you know will come regularly. These will include living expenses – bed, board, food, travel – and essential clothing. It also includes money to pay back credit card bills or overdrafts. None of these bills are things you can put aside without it coming back to bite you.

▶ A second is for savings – money put aside to pay any essential bills that come up unexpectedly such as repair bills.

▶ A third is for saving for fun – for the clothes you want but don't need, or holidays, or expensive events you want to go to but need to plan for.

▶ A fourth is spending money – money in your pocket you can splash around on meals out, coffee to go, a glass of wine with friends and a film.

The lesson is that Money #1 is the non-negotiable bit. If you haven't put aside enough to cover these expenses you're in trouble.

Money #2 is a very good way of making sure you never fall down on payments to anything in the Money #1 category.

Money #3 is the fun part that makes it all worthwhile. Money #3 is the carrot that gives the reward to paying attention and keeping on the straight and narrow with Money #1 and #2.

And Money #4 is what we all want to have – the cash in our pocket to fritter away on little things that make the day worthwhile. The problem is that it adds up alarmingly quickly, and that's the bit we often don't realize. A coffee shop coffee and a snack a day becomes £60 to £70 a month or more – quite a dent in a first time pay cheque.

THE BANK OF MUM AND DAD

Of course, for many young people there is another line of credit that they don't include in the 4 types of money – The Bank of Mum and Dad. It can be very tempting for young people to go on relying on the Bank of Mum and Dad as long as possible, to help with managing their cash. You may agree to pay their mobile phone bills, pick up the loan for a car, put all sorts of expenses on your own bill and in your own name, to protect them and make sure these bills do get paid.

There are two problems with this. One is that if you keep the bill in your name it might mean it always gets paid, but equally it ensures that they never get a credit history. They may apply for a mortgage, a loan or even for a bank account later on and if you've been bankrolling them all these years, they can get refused simply for having no credit history. Help them out by all means when they are young, but the earlier they begin to do things in their own names the better. Just make sure they realize how very, very important it is not to default.

The other problem with their not doing things in their own name is it means they don't get the practice. Managing money is like any other skill – the more you do it and do it successfully, the more competent and confident you become in doing so. Support them, encourage them, urge them to come to you with problems...but warn them that while if they've made a genuine mistake you might rescue them once, you won't bail them out a second time, and stick to that.

Your reservations
Part of your Exit Planning will be to address your own feelings about your children moving out. You'll need to be honest with yourself. Get a piece of paper and make two columns – drawbacks and advantages. With your partner, or on your own, ideas storm and write down all the pluses and minuses you can think of.

Doing this will help you consider how your perception of the minuses might be holding all of you back and look at how you could maximize the advantages to outweigh the drawbacks. If you find you've thought of far more drawbacks than advantages, that's a signal for you to work on your perceptions and expectations. What advantages could you find, to make this a positive development, and help you let go?

Their reservations
Similarly, part of your Exit Planning will be to address their feelings about moving out. You need to help them write down their advantages and disadvantages – and probably discuss the former

to make them more realistic (all night parties every weekend or not having to go to bed before 1 a.m. may not be such a good idea…). Looking at the disadvantages, you may then need to help them with skills and support to make the practical side of looking after themselves something they can feel confident about.

PREPARATION

Preparation for managing for themselves is something you can instil from quite some time before they need to put their exit plan into operation. We've talked about chores as something all children should do from an early age. This is the time when knowing how to run a home will stand them in good stead. Young people who are used to pulling their weight at home and can cook, clean and keep their clothes looking presentable can tick more things off the list of new experiences that can drag them down. If you've not insisted on them making such efforts before, do so now. They may have anxieties about leaving you and your love and care, about coping on their own, about taking on the responsibility of a home of their own; those fears are quite enough to be getting on with without being scared because you have no idea how to prepare food in any other way than to push buttons on a microwave, or how clothes magically go from the floor to the laundry basket to back in the cupboard all clean and pressed.

KEY POINTS

1 The secret to surviving the Empty Nest is to practise for what is about to happen, to deal with your mourning and celebration, to accept change and finally to take action.

2 Take the new opportunity to firmly re-establish your relationship as a couple and then to do as many of the things as possible, large and small, that had to be put in the background while your child was still with you. Don't delay since you might have the role of grandparents to consider in the not too distant future!

3 If you are a single parent, now might be the best time to re-enter the wider world and find yourself new activities, new friends or maybe even a new partner.

4 Keeping contact with your newly flown is a definite balancing act that should suit both parties. Too little can leave the home-leaver feeling unsupported. Too much can stop them feeling able to stand on their own two feet.

5 Letting go is a natural part of life's progress and if it is not done well, it can hinder the young person's natural development. Continuing to treat a young adult in the 'You will always be my little boy/girl' manner will do just that and produce an adult who is really just a grown-up child.

6 Once your young person has left home you will need to renegotiate a new contract with them. The new situation needs new rules, new agreements and boundaries if it is to work without unnecessary friction.

7 A new contract will be even more necessary if the nest-leaver comes back for more than just a visit – the now commonplace 'Boomerang Kids' thrown up by our economically difficult times.

8 How about the ones who don't want to or won't leave? There are four main reasons for this – unrealistic expectations, your needs, their anxieties and difficulty in finding or affording a place to go to. All of these need to be examined and dealt with by both

the parents and the young person if a successful transition from dependence to independence is to be made.

9 Finding and affording a place to go to will be a lot easier if you, or their school, have already taught your offspring about the realities of money in the outside world and have shown them the merits and the techniques of good budgeting. If you haven't done this, bring them back for a crash course in money management.

10 Letting go should be a time of self-congratulation at a hard job done well. See your own 'empty nest' as a place of new opportunities where you can now do some of the things you want to do, and a place where your fledgling will be happy to come back to for many years to come.

BEING HAPPY

How are you doing with the fun sheet? Here are a few more ideas to add – do your own!

Small things	Medium things	Big things
Snuggle up on the sofa with a pet and stroke them. Snuggle up on the sofa with your partner and pet them.	Call and talk with a family member who isn't at home with you. Redecorate a room, or rearrange the furniture.	Go to the races. Visit a garden. Get to know your adult children's partners. Plan an adult only holiday to somewhere you've never been before.

7

The 'sandwich generation' and grandparents

In this chapter you will learn:
- *How parents can be squeezed and pulled between the competing demands of their children and their own parents*
- *The importance of grandparents*
- *About managing living in a three generational household*

Increasingly, just as the boomerang generation of children are refusing to leave home or are coming back, the older generation, those children's grandparents, may also be placing extra demands on their children.

The sandwich generation

The sandwich generation may find it hard not just because of extra demands or work. It's also because they find their identity pulled in two different directions – to be a parent at the same time as falling back into the emotional landscape of a child, with the added discomfort of often finding their own parents demanding a form of parenting from them. Those different pressures and burdens can make the situation and this time stressful.

FAMILY TIES

To understand exactly how difficult these demands are we need to understand the complex web of ties every family has. We are all connected to the people around us. How we lean and rely on partners, our family and friends, and how they count on us, changes as we grow and develop. We call this the Circle of Dependence, because we go from dependence to independence, to interdependence and back again to dependence.

DEPENDENCE

When small our children are entirely dependent on us. Their happiness rests entirely on our ability and willingness to keep them safe and healthy, to feed and wrap them up and make them secure. Perhaps even more important than physical nurturing is the emotional side, as we help them to happiness through love and stimulation so they grow and thrive emotionally and intellectually as well as physically.

INDEPENDENCE

Independence should really begin to be a feature when your child becomes a teenager. Of course, if you've begun handing over some of the reins when they are a child, negotiating when and what to let go of when they are a teenager may be easier. Not only will they be more used to the idea of earning such responsibility but also of the need to show you they can manage. But even if you've kept a tight hold up to now, it's never too late to start and the teenage years are when you'll have to begin to let go, for your sense of happiness as well as your teenager's. Nothing quite raises the stress and tension in a home as a teenager going through the development phase of trying to separate with a parent who won't let go. Teenagers need to show to themselves, their family and the world at large that they can fly on their own, and the best way of acquiring a skill is to practise it.

THE BEGINNINGS OF INTERDEPENDENCE

Once your children have grown past the throes of adolescence you can begin to help them form interdependent relationships with you and others. One of the signs of maturity is to recognize that it's OK – it isn't a sign of weakness but one of strength – to link up with, and even need, other people. Teenagers make fitful forays into this in their early relationships, when they may load everything onto one person who becomes the centre of their focus, pushing friends, interests and necessary tasks such as schoolwork to the side. But one important aspect of interdependence is that it's mutual and reciprocal – as some teenage relationships certainly are, but some are sadly not. And interdependence tends to be part of a network, so that it spreads out from the couple at the heart of one interdependency, to encompass their family and friends. Interdependence isn't exclusive but inclusive and it's what allows you to be yourself at the same time as welcoming a close partnership with another person. In a happy, emotionally warm family we are interdependent with our partners, our adult children, our own parents and others too – friends and colleagues form links with us that sustain and support us all.

OLD AGE AND DEPENDENCE

But one of the important aspects of the circle can be seen in families when the older generation – your parents, your children's grandparents – advance towards the stage of again being dependent. As they age, they may gradually return to needing the daily support of others, to the point of being dependent on them. So one of the difficult situations the sandwich generation may be trying to manage is a balancing act between letting your teenagers go at the same time as becoming more involved in caring for your own parents – reeling one set in as you're letting the other set go. Having to take over some of the responsibility you always saw your own parents managing for themselves, at the same time as needing to revise how much slack you cut your children, can be confusing and frustrating. It often means you have to think carefully about the roles that each person in your life plays and either wants or needs to play. It can mean your having to have conversations with both sides that seem eerily similar.

The importance of grandparents

A family with an old person has a living treasure of gold.

Chinese Proverb

Grandparents can be one of the most important and sustaining aspects of family happiness. Grandparents can supply a steady stream of encouragement and support to both their children and their grandchildren. From the beginning, they can offer welcome advice – after all, necessarily, they been there, done that and got the T-shirt. However, this has to be offered carefully. Sensible and sensitive grandparents know that new parents are vulnerable and insecure. Wanting to protect their self-esteem and project competency new parents may see the offering of advice as interfering. This can be counterproductive, especially for fathers.

Grandparents are such an asset to your children. If you're lucky enough to be on good terms, they're so important for a myriad of reasons. On the practical side, they can give useful parenting suggestions and they do provide a free babysitting and child minder service. Less tangible but far more important they give love, affirmation and encouragement to you and your children. Kids really benefit from having the extra eye, ear and shoulder to lean on. Granddad and Grandma are close enough to give that unconditional love we all need, while being one step away from being parents. This is vital, because what often muddies the waters between parent and child is that everything our children do we often feel reflects on us.

MAKING GRANDPARENT RELATIONSHIPS WORK

Family happiness can often rest on grandparents being an integral part of their grandchildren's upbringing, even if they live a distance away. But in some families, the relationship can be fraught and difficult. Often this is because you and your parents had a tempestuous time together and the bad feeling from this remains. Often it can be because you and your parents have very different ideas about child rearing and you have clashed painfully over it. How can you ensure the relationship lasts and is helpful to all of you?

Top tips

1 Ideas storm what you want and need
   It helps to sit down with your partner and get some clarity on what input you want and need from your parents, and what they might bring to you and your children. Talking it through can help you cut through the traditional expectations and assumptions to reach the issues you'd really value. That might include unconditional love, the knowledge that if you hit a crisis they'd drop everything to be with you, the free babysitting, and the memories from childhood you'd love to have them pass on.

2 Reflect on what might be difficult
   Having ideas stormed the things you'd really find worthwhile, it would help you to identify the things that don't help. These could include the unsolicited advice that only makes you feel pressured or bad, the parenting style you might find too harsh or too lax, unwelcome criticism or an assumption that they can come round anytime without needing to ask.

3 Establish an adult/adult relationship

Once you know what you'd welcome and what you'd prefer to leave out, you can establish a relationship with your parents that is no longer child to parent, where they have the upper hand, but adult to adult, where you meet as equals. Once you have your mind set on achieving this and can pinpoint the triggers that might drive you to behave as a child and could lead to conflict or unhappiness, you can take steps to avoid them.

4 Be clear and honest, and ask for a dialogue

Trying to avoid conflict, but clearly being unhappy about interaction in families, is the quickest way to hurt feelings and end up in arguments. What often happens is we end up making excuses or telling 'white lies' to avoid giving offence when in fact if we'd been honest we might have found common ground. Often if you state the problem and ask for a mutually agreed and acceptable solution you find that in fact the other party is more than happy to do so – they too may even have had your reservations as well and were only waiting for one of you to make a change.

5 Practise damage limitation

If you can't agree – for instance if your parents' idea of discipline is dramatically different from yours, or you don't want them to smoke or give sweets and they can't compromise – you may have to accept some compromises. You might tell your children that you and your parents have different views and have to agree to differ on it – when with them, their rules apply. Or you may have to accept that you can't leave your children with them unsupervised or for any period of time. Or you may ask your parents to come to you rather than take your children to them.

6 Emphasize the positive

If you and your parents do have issues and conflict, one way of managing it is to focus on the good parts of the relationship and what you all get out of it that is helpful, and let the negatives wash over you. It can be instructive, for instance, to consider how your children see it. Sometimes you and the grandparents clash and cannot get on, but grandchild and grandparent see each other in an entirely different light. You might have a shared history that is abrasive or even painful, while your children see only affection and support.

7 Keep in touch to suit you and your kids

It might be important, as part of your ideas storm, to consider how much contact and in what circumstances suit you all.

Children, for instance, may highly value seeing grandparents... as long as it doesn't prevent them from seeing friends or taking part in important events with them. And you too may find there are times when it is really good to see them, but other times when it feels intrusive or inconvenient. It's far better to be upfront than let resentment brew, and burst out in anger and frustration.

8 Recognize their needs too

However, while we're considering grandparents as an asset to you, it's worth recognizing they have a life of their own, too. It's too easy to fall into seeing grandparents as the traditional grey haired little old lady or gentleman, just waiting on the chance to be at your beck and call to help you and see the kids, because they have time on their hands. Grandparents nowadays are just as likely to have a thriving social network, busy working lives and many demands of their own. They may be delighted to see you and their grandchildren, but in their own time and fitting in to their own busy schedule.

JUDGING WHEN INTERDEPENDENCE BECOMES DEPENDENCE

Your parents may be enjoying the payoff of all the financial and emotional investment they have made in you. But equally, they may struggle to keep up with the changes they see in their family and the world at large. Grandparents may welcome the chance to interact with young people, in their own grandchildren or other youngsters, but this can depend on confidence and self-worth and the strength of these relationships. Not all older people are able to have the flexibility to accept different times, different mores and different needs. And as they do get older you may begin to feel the pinch as they need more input from you to manage. Will they have the energy and good health to go on helping you, or will they need your care to go on living independently? Or will you have to make judgements and have the conversations about what might be best for all of you, or even make the decisions about their care? As people age they will slip gradually from independence through interdependence and into a new stage of dependence, and it's often difficult to see when they can no longer manage on their own and you need to support or even step in and insist on a new arrangement.

Three generational households

Western developed societies may be almost unique in time and place in separating families as much as they do. The concept of it being the norm for a household to contain parents and their children, and no-one else, is actually quite unusual, in global and historical terms. In other cultures and at other times, the household with children and adults of all ages living together is and was far more common. Four recent developments may be beginning to create a drift back to the idea of three – or even more – generations living together under one roof.

- ▶ Recession
- ▶ Anxiety about the quality of care homes
- ▶ Single parents
- ▶ Other cultures as an example

PLANNING IN ADVANCE

You may be leaving the decision until your own parents or the parent left behind after a bereavement is in crisis and needing care. Or you may be considering it simply because of financial considerations or family needs. Or it may be a subject to consider ahead of time so that when the moment comes, decisions are not made in haste, by default or in the face of protest. If you're thinking about having three generations in the same house, how best can you make it work?

See the positives. Ideas storm together as a family to work out what living together might do for all of you. It might be grandparents on tap for the kids – a chance to always have at least one adult willing to give them time and attention, and unconditional love. It might be another adult on hand with advice or as someone to bounce ideas off for you. It could be a way of making sure there is always someone extra to help and thus ensure conflict is lessened and fun is maximized. And of course it might mean protection and help for them when they need it.

Explore the negatives. Jumping or even sliding slowly into a new way of doing things is likely to end in disaster if you haven't considered the drawbacks. However happy all of you are about the situation there are bound to be points of difference or conflict and ignoring them until they come up tends to mean they build until they assume epic proportions. And if there is conflict already, trying to ignore it will not mean it goes away. So explore why and how you might disagree and look for ways of compromising and coming to agreement.

Set rules and guidelines. Just as you might have with your children, call a Family Round Table and ideas storm the rules and guidelines you'd like your new unit to run by. You may want to agree times to be apart and together, ways of being able to say 'I love you but need some space now...' and how you will dovetail different ways of doing things.

Respect each other's space. If you have to share rooms agree times when you each go out to leave kitchen and living room to the other, and times you will share; agree also how you'll draw it to each other's attention if you need to talk it through and change the arrangement. Agree territorial rights on separate rooms – both children and adults may need to consider and find ways of enforcing privacy. Everyone may need to agree to knock and wait until invited, and not to enter other people's rooms when they are not there.

Respect each other's way of doing things and don't impose. Different generations and just different people have different ways of managing various issues – how you discipline your children, what you consider to be healthy food, what importance you put on housework. You may need to discuss these and come to a working compromise.

Share playtime. When you live together sometimes you forget to go out together. Just as couples should make dates with each other, various members of a family living under the same roof should make a point of having treats together too, outside and at home. You all may benefit from agreed nights out in various combinations, and nights where you cook together and play board games or watch a TV programme you all enjoy together. You will also benefit from agreeing times when you will go your separate ways, to give all of you a rest from each other.

Share worktime. Play together but also do the essential things round the house together. As they get older grandparents may find it harder to keep up with maintenance but be inclined to let it go rather than admit to having problems. If you've established a routine of certain times in the week when everyone mucks in and does certain chores, and picks up the slack for those in the family who have genuine problems, when it's really necessary it will be second nature. Even small children and arthritic oldies can do something when they feel part of a group effort.

Don't let a problem grow. If you have an issue, call a family conference or sit down quietly with the other person and air it calmly. Confront the problem not the person and ask 'How can we sort this so everyone is happy?'

KEY POINTS

1 Being a part of the 'sandwich generation', with demands both from grown children and elderly parents of your own, is now a growing phenomenon in today's society – and can be very hard work.

2 To deal with the various demands of this situation, we must understand the Circle of Dependence – how we move in life from a child's dependence to an adult's independence and interdependence, and then back again to elderly dependence.

3 This, in turn, means that we need to understand the complex web of ties every family has and how we are all connected to other people around us.

4 The number of balls the sandwich generation has to keep juggling can vary. At its most stressful this could mean letting your young person go while attending to your elderly parents' needs while trying to deal with your own emotions about the empty nest while going through a mid-life crisis of your own.

5 Not all the elderly are a problem and most can be a definite asset to the sandwich generation.

6 Grandparents can be one of the sustaining aspects of family happiness and can be a steady source of support and encouragement to both their children and their grandchildren. This can be particularly important if the family has been divided by separation or loss.

7 Grandparents should be valued and involved. They have a great deal to offer, often far more than just being babysitters.

8 To get the best of your grandparent asset you might need to renegotiate your status with them. You are no longer child and parent but adult and adult. You should now meet as equals.

9 You and your parents will not agree about everything – discipline, treats and some manners or habits, for example. Some compromises can be settled by joint discussions and establishing some ground rules.

10 With negotiation and compromise, being part of the sandwich
    generation can be more like a warm family embrace than a
    painful and inescapable bear hug.

BEING HAPPY

How are you doing with the fun sheet? Here are a few more ideas to
add – do your own!

Small things	Medium things	Big things
Look through family photos with kids and grandparents. Appreciate being greeted by your family pet as if you've been away for months, even though it was ten minutes. Start a new tube of toothpaste or bottle of shampoo.	Enjoy the relationship you can have with adult kids – and their relationship with each other. Finding the cake you left that morning in the tin is still there because there are no ravening kids in the house. Sitting in the garden or on a park bench to watch a spectacular sunset.	A glass of wine on a patio in Greece or France or somewhere else hot. Walking on a beach at sunrise. Seeing the Northern Lights. Having my adult child tell me they are getting engaged.

Separations and new unions

In this chapter you will learn:
- *To understand how children feel about family change*
- *About putting children first*
- *The importance of keeping contact between children and both parents*

I'd like to think that happy families stay together, happily. But the reality is that more and more families are breaking up and re-forming. One question I often get asked as an agony aunt is 'How can we make sure our children are not affected by our separation?'

The answer is, of course, you can't. Any change in a family is hard to process and manage. This is true whether it's change that is natural and expected, such as children growing up and moving from primary to secondary school, or leaving home to go to college or to start first jobs. It is true whether the change is common but perhaps unexpected such as illness or death and the loss of someone close. Whether change is traumatic or welcome it poses challenges, but what it never does is leave people unaffected.

Family change hurts children whatever age they may be

Family change in the sense of the breakdown of an original family and the establishment of a new one is probably the hardest for children to manage. And that is true whether children are toddlers, school age, teenagers or even grown up and married with their own kids. It's a child's worst nightmare that their parents separate. It may be your solution to a problem, and it might be the best result for all involved. But you cannot find a way of it not being something that will hurt and challenge them.

But the hopeful news is that it would seem that it's not so much **that** your family breaks up and re-forms that is the problem, but **how** you do it. Both adults and children can come through family change with self-esteem and self-confidence intact. They can continue having a mother and a father who love them and are there for them, and go on to have as good and as happy outcomes in their lives as families who stay together. But it takes both awareness and work for this to happen.

How do you make a break-up as bearable as possible? Perhaps the best advice is contained in once sentence:

Love Your Children More than You Hate each Other.

It's as simple as that. However hurt and angry you are you should approach all discussions and all plans for separation with the effect it might have on your children in mind. That doesn't mean you should 'stay together for the sake of the children' which can often be every bit if not more devastating to them as separation. What it means is:

▶ Having and ending the argument.
▶ Agreeing to move from being partners to co-parents.
▶ Making a Parenting Plan to co-parent your children.

Having and ending the argument
Bitterness and resulting conflict tend to continue because you don't finish the argument between you. Both parents/ex-partners may be left with the feeling that the other person hasn't heard – how angry you are, how let down, how sad. The nasty, niggly digs that continue to be made, often through the kids, are all about continuing an attempt to feel your partner knows what it is you want to say to them. It's far more efficient and far, far kinder to the children if you both give each other the opportunity to speak, and be heard. And that's best done with a counsellor (see Taking it further) who can help each of you both to speak and to listen, and keep the peace.

Agreeing to move from being partners to co-parents
Once you can draw a line under your argument you might be able to move on to being co-parents. You can agree to no longer being

partners to each other, but if you have children you do have, always shall have and should have a connection. Your children deserve both parents. Unless the other parent is unsafe, your children need to see them and be in contact. Even then, you might consider letting contact happen in the safety of a Children's Contact Centre, under supervision. Contact should not be once a month or in holidays – it should be daily and as far as possible in the child's control. With modern technology, this is easy, as long as one parent does not assume the role of gatekeeper. Once you have moved on from your argument by using a counsellor, you might like to use a mediator to help you agree the details of how to co-parent.

Making a Parenting Plan to co-parent your children
You can download an excellent publication that covers all the ins and outs of separated but co-parenting (www.cafcass.gov.uk/PDF/FINAL%20web%20version%20251108.pdf). It helps you discuss and agree a way of supporting your children in thinking well of both parents and having full access to both, and in helping the two of you make common ground all the important issues – day to day arrangements, money, holidays, school, religion, health, family issues and much more.

Children's needs

When approaching a separation one important thing to keep in mind is that it is an adult solution to an adult problem. Yes, your children may be suffering from conflict and arguments at home, the spinoff of your relationship having problems. And they may in consequence be in conflict with you. And indeed in some cases they may have just as much of a disagreement with one of the adults involved as does the other. But the reality often is that children have no reason to want either parent to be out of their lives or indeed for the relationship to break down and break up. They would far, far rather you could end the problems and remain together. If you separate it's your choice, not theirs. So while they may feel relief as a split brings an end to some arguments and feel glad for you if you are in a better place, you and they may well have one marked difference in approaching this situation: you want it, they do not. This can lead to conflict and misunderstanding if you are assuming they feel the same as you do, and they don't. You are the adult and have every right to have the buck stop with you, and make decisions that you feel are right for you and your children. But it may be necessary to at least acknowledge that they feel differently.

New unions

Similarly, when approaching a new partnership, you need to be aware that your perspective and your child's are very different. What might be a new and joyful beginning for adults can be a horrible and opposed ending for children. Your new relationship puts the nail in the coffin for their hopes that their original family might get back together again. In response, they can often act out their misery and anger in bad behaviour. And this is true even if they had every reason to be happy that what went before is over – either a long period with you struggling as a single parent or a family with conflict and anger.

With eyes fixed on different things, children and adults can come into conflict and misunderstand each other's behaviour and reactions. The main issues in stepfamilies can be seen thus:

A stepfamily is always the result of someone's loss.

Somebody has to have died or a family has to have come apart for a stepfamily to begin.

A stepfamily can be a second chance for everyone involved.

On the positive side, a second family can be a chance for both adults and children to try again – including the adults now living apart – and do better this time. Parents who might not have done as well as they might while living with their own children can realize what they are missing and try harder once apart.

Unfinished business and baggage

However a family ends, you'll always be left with unfinished business. There will be anger, guilt, hurt, jealousy and all sorts of feelings left over from the split and the aftermath. This baggage is carried over to the new family, often creating barriers between members and lasting reservations and conflict. Unfinished business or baggage will not disappear if ignored. Brushing stuff under the carpet simply forms a bump you'll keep tripping over.

The package deal

You can't cherry pick; children come too. If you form a relationship with someone who has children you can't expect that relationship to be between the adults only. And if you go into a relationship with children of your own, you shouldn't see your partnership with the new adult as a separate issue to your relationship with your children. Whether children live with you full time or only visit – or even if they are not in contact – they are still a full-time part of the new relationship and have to be taken into account. Anyone who can't accept this really should not be entering into a relationship where there are children.

> **Insight**
>
> Adults can divorce; children can't. Children may, in pain and rage, cut off contact with a parent after a separation. But the reality is that since you have been there all their lives, both of you are fixtures for them. Adults can edit an ex-partner out of their own lives because you had a life before they came along – you remain separate individuals. Children have their parents as part of their foundation and bedrock – it's really traumatic and damaging to divorce yourself from that.

Loving children not our own

All our natural instincts fight against making another person's child 100 per cent our own, which is why it can be difficult to become emotionally linked to them. Lions kill the offspring of their rivals when they take over a pride. We don't go that far, although some people fantasize about it! What we need to do is at least recognize that while you may fall in love with an adult, you often don't fall in love with their children, who are the living, breathing, walking proof that someone was there and loved before you. It's not unusual then to feel no affection, and some antipathy, for them. What you should not do is show it or act it out. Adults are the grownups here; it's up to us to do our best to make the relationship work and to understand and allow for some negative feelings and behaviour from children.

Losing touch

One in two fathers lose touch with their children within two years of a separation.

Frequently, this is not because of any lack of love or wish not to be in contact. Fathers tend to lose touch for several reasons. One may be that so many barriers are put in the way of the relationship that they give up. Often, they feel that the whole situation is so fraught and painful they can't cope. They may well believe they are doing the best thing for their children by removing themselves as a source of friction. Another is their own feelings of incompetence – they believe they are not good at being fathers and can't see a way of improving. Fathers' relationships with their own children are often encouraged, maintained and mediated by the mother. When she is not putting any effort into supporting it, it can fall by the wayside.

Losing contact with a parent will always leave a hole in a child's life.

Children will always feel bereft if a father goes out of their lives. They may have a conflicted relationship together, but he's still dad. Sons tend to model themselves on their dads, and daughters model their relationships with men on their relationship with their father. Both can have their feelings of self-worth significantly damaged by a father, or mother, leaving their lives.

Discipline and acting out

Children can lose any sense of control over their own life when a family breaks up.

It wasn't their choice, so children can feel spectacularly powerless when a family break-up happens. Since kids tend to think the world revolves around them, they may well get the idea it was their fault – if only they had done something, or not done something, maybe it wouldn't have happened. Control may become a big issue – they may do all sorts of things to kick against what you want or say, to try and feel as if they have some.

Bad behaviour, as we have already discussed, is the way we 'act out' feelings. When children behave badly, you always need to ask 'What has happened to trigger this?' If we're feeling sad, mad or bad, we can very rarely sit down and calmly say 'I say, Mum and Dad, I feel awful about what is happening.' Instead, we shout and argue and fight and generally show what we are feeling through our actions.

So how can we help our family come through the establishing of a new family in as effective and happy a way as possible?

Recognize the loss

Recognize the loss involved in your gain, and allow children the opportunity to voice their feelings and anxieties. Expressing reservations or anger doesn't create or harden such feelings – it allows them to be voiced and in doing so, brought under control. Negative feelings once voiced and heard by you often lessen.

Deal with unfinished business.

Recognize how left-over anger and arguments can affect everyone, bring them out into the open and take opportunities for professional help to manage them.

Locate anger where it belongs.

Family conflict often happens because we direct anger at the people around us when we're really upset with people not present – missing people in our lives or people from our past. So we can be angry at a child when it's a parent or someone from our own childhood who has really triggered the upset. Talking with a counsellor can often help us put the anger where it belongs and so manage it.

Accept the package deal

Recognize that for a stepfamily to work everyone has to accept the presence of the children involved, and work to make that relationship function. But it can take time and effort to build a relationship – be patient and supportive of everyone.

Keep in touch

Children will always miss the parent they do not live with, however that parent might have behaved and however bad a parent they may be. Unless we are talking real risk of harm – and even then, it can be managed – children deserve and need continuing contact with both parents. Sometimes people can be really awful partners, but good parents.

Help contact to be maintained

Missing family members need the support of everyone involved to stay in touch and do their best. Making it difficult may feel satisfying as it hurts your ex-partner but you have to recognize: the people most hurt by this will be the children. Love Your Children More Than You Hate Each Other.

Recognize bad behaviour is about bad feelings.

If children are acting up it is because they are acting out. The only question to ask is 'What is this really about, and what can I do about it?' Once the real source of angst is put into words and is out in the open, bad behaviour usually improves. Instead of punishing them we need to give them a voice, and look for solutions to the problems their behaviour is showing.

KEY POINTS

1 Ideally, families should stay together happily but the reality is that more and more are breaking up and re-forming.

2 A separation is an adult's solution to an adult's problem. But to a child, it's the worst nightmare and everything possible must be done to guide them through this emotional time.

3 There is one way to make the break-up more bearable to a child – love them more than you hate each other!

4 Bitterness and conflict can continue in a separating couple if arguments have not been resolved fully. Counselling can help by giving both of you the opportunity to have your full say, and to listen to your ex-partner.

5 When considering a new relationship after a separation or a loss, you need to be aware that yours and your child's perspective will be very different. It may be a new beginning for you, but to them it is another reminder of an ending and a painful loss.

6 Somebody will have had to have died or a family has had to come apart for a stepfamily to begin.

7 However a family ends, there will always be some unfinished business left. This baggage can carry across to the new family and, unless dealt with, can create barriers and conflict. Again, counselling can help.

8 All our natural instincts fight against making another person's child 100 per cent our own. It's not uncommon to feel little affection, and even some antipathy at first. But it is up to the adults to make the best of things and to expect and allow for some negative feelings and behaviour from the children. In time, affection and a relationship can grow, if you give it time and effort.

9 Losing contact with a parent will always leave a hole in a child's life. So unless there is a risk of harm, and even this can be managed by a supervision agency, children need and deserve continuing contact with both parents.

10 Second families can, and do, work happily. It's a case of always putting the children first – the situation, whether from loss or separation, is not their fault, nor of their making. The good news is that, done properly, second families can and do work happily.

For more on this complex situation you might like to see my book on the subject, *Be A Great Step-parent* in the Teach Yourself series.

BEING HAPPY

How are you doing with the fun sheet? Here are a few more ideas to add – do your own!

Small things	Medium things	Big things
A cold drink on a hot day. A hot chocolate on a freezing day. Warm socks straight out of the dryer. That fresh smell just after a rainstorm.	A new article of clothing, first time on. An unexpected compliment. When you leave work on the beginning of a long bank holiday weekend. Chatting with someone on a train journey and really getting on well.	Realizing after a crisis that it is getting better. First morning of a holiday when the whole break stretches in front of you. Going bowling.

A final word

Happiness can often be easier to find than we might think. It's often simply a question of balance. Of recognizing priorities and choosing, more often than not, to go with the options that afford you time with your family and others you value, a chance to build the bonds between you and to enjoy yourselves.

Here are some tips to help you make that balance work for you.

Make room for couple and me time
You need time together, and also time doing the things you enjoy. Both tend to get shoved to the side when your children are growing up and demanding your time and attention. Don't miss out – put dates together, and some time for yourself, in your diary. If you don't you won't, and if you don't you and your relationship will suffer. It doesn't have to be spontaneous to be romantic.

Quality is more important than quantity
Even a quick five minutes together is better than nothing, and lots of five minutes add up. So too do text messages, emails, quick phone calls in the day – anything that keeps you in touch and talking.

This too shall pass
There will be times when time is in really short supply – when kids, jobs, all sorts of calls on you take their toll. You can't alter the short supply of time, but accepting it's the reality of that moment, and will change some time in the future, makes it easier to manage.

Prioritize
If you're running on the spot and feeling really squeezed, take a hard look at your priorities. What is really more important? With a clear eye you may be able to cut out some activities that looked vital but are ultimately less important than others. After all, it's your family and relationship at stake and surely they come first?

Get Help
Don't feel you have to do it all yourself. Share chores around the family, rope in friends and family to baby/childsit, ask your mother-in-law to do the ironing (or use non-iron clothes) give up a night out

to pay for a cleaner. Again, think about what is really important – a wonderful evening laughing your head off with your children that you will remember for the rest of your lives... or that there are no dust bunnies under the beds. I'd keep the dust bunnies.

Perfection is not a happy trait
It's better to let your standards slip than your relationship or your family's happiness. Any meal tastes better when it's eaten together, and you can't see the clutter by candlelight.

Full cup...
It's also OK to do things for ourselves – sometimes we need to give ourselves permission to take some time to treat ourselves and fill that cup. When we do we relax, charge our batteries, feel better about ourselves and our children, feel better about life, and are more able to cope. And nurturing ourselves helps us take better care of our children, and our partner. What we need to remember, for our own and everyone in our family's happiness is that everyone's needs are important – yours, your partner's, your children's and the needs of other family members.

Keep this in mind: Be Happy!

Taking it further

The Samaritans

The Samaritans are available 24-hours a day to listen to people in distress and to provide emotional support.

www.samaritans.org

email: jo@samaritans.org

Helpline: 08457 90 90 90

FURTHER HELP: LIST OF ORGANIZATIONS PROVIDING HELP IN PARENTING AND FAMILY ISSUES

British Association for Counselling and Psychotherapy

The association can suggest a counsellor in your area online at their website or via post.

www.bacp.co.uk

Care For The Family

Care for the Family is a national charity which aims to promote strong family life and to help those who face family difficulties.

www.careforthefamily.org.uk/

DadTalk and dad.info

An online community for fathers with help, advice, forums and features.

Families and Friends of Lesbians and Gays (FFLAG)

Provides information and support for parents of lesbian, gay and bisexual young people and their families.

www.fflag.org.uk

Families Need Fathers

A registered charity providing information and support on shared parenting issues arising from family breakdown to divorced and separated parents.

www.fnf.org.uk

Family Lives

The national charity that offers help and support in all aspects of family lives.

www.familylives.org.uk

Family Mediators Association

Can put you in touch with trained mediators who work with both parents and children.

www.thefma.co.uk

Gingerbread

Provide a helpline with free information to lone parents.

www.gingerbread.org.uk

Grandparents' Association

www.grandparents-association.org.uk

Helpline: 0845 4349585

NSPCC

The NSPCC can help with advice on keeping your or any other child safe.

www.nspcc.org.uk

PAPYRUS (Parents' Association for the Prevention of Young Suicide)

Provides information and advice for parents, teachers and healthcare professionals.

www.papyrus.org.uk

Relate

Offers relationship counselling and life-skills courses through local Relate centres.

www.relate.org.uk

Separated Dads

A website containing articles and advice for dads living away from their children and offering a regular email newsletter.

www.separateddads.co.uk/

The Institute of Family Therapy

The institute helps with family problems.

www.instituteoffamilytherapy.org.uk

Index